The UK Cider Industry

Profiles of the leading 400 companies

John D Blackburn

Editor

First Edition

Spring 2019

ISBN-13: 978-1-912736-12-6

ISBN-10: 1-912736-12-8

All rights reserved. No part of this publication may be reproduced, distributed, or transmitted in any form or by any means, including photocopying, recording, or other electronic or mechanical methods, without our prior written permission, except in the case of brief quotations embodied in critical reviews and certain other non-commercial uses permitted by copyright law. For permission requests, please write to us.

Copyright © 2019 Dellam Publishing Limited

Printed in 8pt Nimbus Sans L

Designed by URW++ Design and Development GmbH

Dellam Publishing Limited

2 Heath Drive, Sutton, Surrey, SM2 5RP

Fax: 020 8770 7478   email: enquiries@dellam.com

SAN: 0177881   EAN/GLN: 5030670177882

Table of Contents

1 Acknowledgements iv

2 Introduction v

3 Total Assets League Table 1

- As a measure of size, total assets is preferable to turnover which is influenced by profit margins and whether companies are capital or labour intensive.

4 Age of Companies 5

- Each company is ranked by its date of incorporation. Newcomers are defined as those registered since 2017.

5 Geographic Distribution 9

- Each company is classed by county.

6 Company Profiles 13

- Full company name, date incorporated, net worth, total assets, registered office, activities, shareholders and parent company, directors (with date of birth, nationality and occupation) and number of employees (if available).

7 Index of Directorships 39

- Alphabetical list of directors showing their directorships. If several directors have identical names then their date of birth is shown.

8 Standard Industrial Classification 51

- These codes are used to classify businesses by the type of economic activity in which they are engaged.

9 *finis* 55

Acknowledgements

This is a long and detailed publication containing thousands of facts and figures. It is only to be expected, despite continuous and repeated editing and checking, that errors may occur. In such cases, once we are aware of any, we publish a correction on our website.

Readers are encouraged to check regularly at www.dellam.com/books for any corrections and updates.

Although we take extreme care to ensure accuracy and being up-to-date, we cannot accept responsibility for any errors or omissions.

Contains public sector information licensed under Open Government Licence v3.0. from The Charity Commission (England and Wales) and The Charity Commission for Northern Ireland. © Crown Copyright and database right (2018).

Contains information from the Scottish Charity Register supplied by the Office of the Scottish Charity Regulator and licensed under the Open Government Licence v.2.0. © Crown Copyright and database right (2018).

Contains OS data © Crown copyright and database right (2018)

Contains Royal Mail data © Royal Mail copyright and database right (2018)

Contains National Statistics data © Crown copyright and database right (2018)

Contains Office for National Statistics © Crown copyright and database right (2018)

Maps based on those produced by the Office for National Statistics Geography GIS & Mapping Unit (2012 and 2018).

Contains HM Land Registry data © Crown copyright and database right (2018).

Contains Parliamentary information licensed under the Open Parliament Licence v3.0.

House of Commons Library Briefing Papers licensed under the Open Parliament Licence v3.0.

Contains Food Standards Agency data © Crown copyright and database right (2018).

Contains Eurostat data, 1995-2018, copyright European Commission by the Decision of 12 December 2011.

Maps based on produced by ONS Geography GIS & Mapping Unit.

Contains Companies House data supplied under section 47 and 50 of the Copyright, Designs and Patents Act 1988 and Schedule 1 of the Database Regulations (SI 1997/3032).

We appreciate your interest in our publications, and your comments and suggestions are always welcome. Please contact us at enquiries@dellam.com.

Introduction

This study looks at all companies registered in the United Kingdom where they identify themselves as manufacturers of cider and other fruit wines.

This study includes companies that are dormant or non-trading some of which might be latent while others may operate under their owners' names but are incorporated to protect the business name. In addition, all newly incorporated companies are included. The study will exclude those companies that do not specifically identify themselves as manufacturers of cider and other fruit wines.

The aim of this study is to provide an overview of the key movers and shakers in the UK cider and other fruit wines sector. Only key data has been isolated, particularly the company's net worth and total assets, but also its full name, date incorporated, registered office, other activities, shareholders, directors (with date of birth, occupation and nationality) and number of employees.

Two indicators of size are used: net worth and total assets. These are preferable to turnover which is influenced by profit margins and whether the companies are capital or labour intensive.

In the years 2016, 2017 and 2018, new company incorporations in this sector were 48, 49 and 90 respectively.

In Great Britain, 57% of those aged 16 years and over in 2017 drank alcohol (29 million people of the population) while 20% did not drink alcohol at all.

NACM Cider Makers Limited is the trade body as well as the South West of England Cidermakers' Association (SWECA). L'Association des Industries des Cidres et Vins de Fruits de l'U.E. (A.I.C.V.) represents the European Union cider and fruit wine industries located in Brussels.

UK cider represents 39% of the global market and is worth £3 billion in the UK. The rest of Europe accounts for 25% of global sales. The market is dominated by H P Bulmer Limited and Magners GB Limited. Cider represents 7% of total alcohol sales with exports representing £100 million.

The market's annual growth is just over 2%. Some 64% is sold off trade through supermarkets. Cider has grown 3.5% in value and 2.2% in volume over the last year. While pear cider continues to decline, losing over 20% volume while crafted cider has grown by 17%.

The growth of the cider market is driven by a demand for gluten-free drinks and a preference for low alcohol beverages. However, its high sugar content is the major factor that hampers growth.

More than 11,000 pubs have closed in the UK in the last decade, a fall of almost a quarter (23%). The number of UK pubs has fallen from around 52,500 in 2001 to some 38,815 in 2018. Although many pubs have closed, the total turnover of pubs and bars has held up, remaining flat since 2008, adjusting for inflation.

Standard cataloguing guidelines for company names in the profile section have been used, but there will be occurrences when the name may not be strictly alphabetical. A certain licence was adopted where it was felt that strictly alphabetical could lead to improper cataloguing. Some company names have been shortened in the league tables for aesthetic reasons.

John D Blackburn
Editor

This page is intentionally left blank

Total Assets League Table

Company	Revenue	Company	Revenue
H P Bulmer Limited	£182,007,000	Robinsons Cider Limited	£396,674
Magners GB Limited	£169,904,000	Torre Cider Co Ltd	£379,349
Halewood International Limited	£97,916,000	Tutts Clump Cider Ltd	£314,501
Brothers Drinks Co. Limited	£72,885,224	Medlar Management Limited	£303,026
Aston Manor Limited	£55,704,092	Saxby Farms Limited	£274,484
Thatchers Cider Company Limited	£52,640,336	Pearsons Ciderworks Ltd	£268,098
Merrydown PLC	£51,247,252	The Cotswold Cider Company Ltd	£259,583
H.Weston & Sons Limited	£42,667,464	White Heron Brands Limited	£258,350
Broadland Wineries Limited	£24,202,070	Ty Gwyn Cider Limited	£209,667
Thomas Hardy Holdings Limited	£19,423,000	Mount Bank Farm Limited	£206,694
Distell International Holdings Limited	£18,152,844	Celtic Marches Beverages Ltd	£203,197
Bevisol Limited	£13,857,646	The Kinross Brewery Limited	£202,786
H & A Prestige Bottling Limited	£11,142,000	Wibblers Brewery (Farms) Limited	£187,463
Cornish Scrumpy Holdings Limited	£10,185,911	Bridge Farm Cider Limited	£186,605
Thomas Hardy Kendal Limited	£9,162,000	Oliver's Cider and Perry Limited	£186,570
Thomas Hardy Burtonwood Limited	£6,525,000	Liberty Orchards Limited	£169,754
H.Mount & Sons Limited	£5,440,523	Lines Brew Co Ltd	£167,946
Lyme Bay Cider Company Limited	£5,223,414	Hunt's Cider Limited	£159,650
Branded Drinks Ltd	£3,886,575	Harry's Cider Company Limited	£159,295
Cornish Scrumpy Company Limited	£3,795,550	The Wessex Wild Plum Company Limited	£156,598
Sheppy's Cider Limited	£3,427,815	Gwatkin Cider Co. Limited	£156,326
The Orchard Pig Ltd	£3,199,530	Cranes Drink Ltd	£153,917
Cornish Orchards Ltd	£2,721,597	Penton Park Brewery Limited	£153,757
Lilley's Cider Limited	£2,567,968	Heron Valley Cider Limited	£148,672
Showerings Cider Mill Ltd	£2,506,517	Himachal Ltd	£145,558
Henney's Cider Company Limited	£2,352,033	Whin Hill (Norfolk) Cider Ltd	£136,568
Cornish Mead Co.Limited	£1,858,961	The Boutique Cellar Limited	£128,656
Thistly Cross Cider Co Limited	£1,541,614	Primeflow Limited	£128,051
Sandford Orchards Limited	£1,345,649	Marsh Barton Farm Cyder Limited	£123,735
Hartpury Heritage Trust	£1,200,023	Long Meadow Cider Ltd	£119,767
Gwynt y Ddraig Cider Ltd	£1,099,830	Umbrella Brewing Limited	£115,512
New Forest Cider Limited	£922,869	Dudda's Tun Ltd	£114,328
Dunkertons Cider Company Limited	£881,020	Overtone Brewing Ltd	£112,528
Perry's Cider Limited	£875,308	Ross-on-Wye Cider & Perry Company Limited	£108,212
Hawkes Cider Limited	£873,412	Apple County Cider Co Limited	£104,675
Marches Bottling and Packaging Limited	£871,052	Hampshire Downs Fine Cider Company Ltd	£101,589
Haygrove Evolution Limited	£842,315	The Regal Rogue Group UK Limited	£100,893
Biddenden Vineyards Limited	£830,730	Scrumpy Wasp Limited	£97,664
Zymurgorium Ltd	£765,763	Abbiss Drinks Company Limited	£95,053
Mac Ivors Cider Co. Limited	£714,521	Brogdale Craft Cider Limited	£92,114
Armagh Cider Company Ltd	£608,039	Hiken Limited	£91,612
Lyme Bay Winery Limited	£600,034	Napton Cidery Limited	£90,495
Bensons Fruit Juice Limited	£590,317	Severn Cider Ltd	£89,528
Hogan's Cider Limited	£570,278	Kent Cider Company Ltd	£89,380
Broughton Ales Limited	£502,688	East Norfolk Trading Company Limited	£89,140
Cairn O'Mohr Ltd.	£481,999	The Harrogate Cider Company Limited	£88,584
Mr. Whitehead's Cider Company Ltd	£474,358	Tiddly Pommes Ltd	£80,733
Ashridge Cider Limited	£458,463	Worleys Cider Limited	£74,212
Broadoak Cider Company Limited	£457,775	Chucklehead Cider Ltd	£71,706
The Garden Cider Company Limited	£440,612	The Orgasmic Cider Co. Ltd	£69,786
The London Beer Company Limited	£438,913	Tempted Cider Company Limited	£65,519
The Lambswick Drinks Co Limited	£421,752	Honey & Daughter Limited	£65,419
The Purbeck Cider Company Limited	£411,010	The Sussex South Downs Company Ltd	£62,324
Whin Hill Cider Limited	£402,579	Cornwall Cider Co. Limited	£62,024

The UK Cider Industry

Company	Amount	Company	Amount
Ashover Cider Company Limited	£60,520	Giggler Ltd	£14,038
Nightingale Cider Company Limited	£60,279	3CS Cider Limited	£12,645
Wise Owl Cider Ltd	£58,973	Parsonage Farm (Croscombe) Ltd	£12,232
DJ Wines Limited	£57,362	L. McCoy Drinks Limited	£12,080
Harnser Enterprises Ltd	£53,813	Revenant Cider Limited	£11,791
St Ives Cider Limited	£53,562	Darley Abbey Cider Company Limited	£11,678
Meon Valley Cider Ltd	£50,941	Pips Cider Limited	£11,476
The Ledbury Cider and Juice Co. Limited	£49,300	Missing Link Brewing Ltd	£11,439
North Coast Cider Company Limited	£46,046	Lancashire Cider Limited	£11,181
Mabinogion Mead Company Limited	£45,688	Secret Orchard Cider Ltd	£9,803
Severn Events Ltd	£45,224	Spinney Abbey Ltd	£9,739
Broxbourne Brewery Ltd.	£44,894	Old Town Brewery Ltd.	£9,611
Legiste Limited	£44,426	The Peasmarsh Cider Company Limited	£8,463
Wessex Cider Limited	£43,712	Vachery Farm Cider Limited	£8,382
The Donhead Apple Company Ltd	£43,592	Hartpury Process Limited	£8,381
Ascension Cider Co. Limited	£41,539	Dee Ciders Limited	£7,398
The Bottle Kicking Cider Company Limited	£40,824	Wadys Cider Limited	£7,365
Handmade Cider Company Limited	£40,447	Horse Kick Cider Ltd	£7,217
Colemans Cider Company Limited	£38,398	Creoda's Hill Ltd	£5,509
Moss Cider Limited	£38,295	Duckchicken Limited	£5,437
Ralph's Cider Ltd	£37,385	Wasted Apple Co Ltd	£5,265
The Husthwaite Orchard Village Limited	£36,444	Tees Cider Ltd	£5,261
Proasset Limited	£34,875	Sherborne Cider Ltd	£5,223
Old Chads Orchard Ltd	£33,729	Tip Tap & Top Ltd	£5,124
Iford Cider Limited	£32,760	Lisnisky Cider Company Ltd	£4,944
Kingscote Winery Ltd	£32,213	Toby's Cider Limited	£4,612
House Brewery Limited	£32,133	The Meanwood Brewery Ltd	£4,372
Pembrokeshire Cider Limited	£31,168	Bygumpty Limited	£4,238
The Southey Brewing Company Limited	£30,692	Duxford Scrumpy Company Limited	£3,733
Pilango Limited	£28,073	The Radnage Cider Company Ltd	£3,723
Analytical-Solutions UK Ltd	£27,473	Stockmoor Cider Limited	£3,618
King Offa Ltd	£26,521	The Fermentorium Ltd	£3,308
Kingswood Cider Limited	£25,722	Apple Hoarders Limited	£3,176
Ashgrove Farm Produce Ltd	£25,710	Pomona Orchards Ltd	£1,965
Olde Mill Ltd	£25,614	Highworth Cider and Perry Limited	£1,706
The Copse House Cider Company Ltd	£25,231	Organic Country Drinks Ltd	£1,449
Chalice Mead Limited	£24,815	Bullington End Cider Limited	£1,153
Caledonia Cider Limited	£23,879	White Rose Cider Limited	£1,026
Marron (Lincoln) Ltd	£23,794	Essex Cider Company Limited	£1,000
Harleston Cider Company Limited	£23,330	The Big Bear Cider Mill Limited	£702
Cidre Bouche UK Limited	£22,500	Brewers Folly Brewery Ltd.	£593
Ham Hill Cider Limited	£21,862	Samba Cidra Ltd	£550
Virtual Orchard Limited	£20,252	SMSNaughton Ltd.	£492
Lyne Down Organics Limited	£20,077	Pennine Cider Limited	£391
Beard and Sabre Ltd.	£17,685	Thompstone Industries Ltd.	£200
The Cotswold Fruit Company Ltd.	£17,607	Frampton Farm Limited	£187
Hoar Cross Cider Ltd	£16,263	The Malmesbury Cider Company Ltd	£100
Broadlands Cider Farm Limited	£14,458	Lost Boys Brewery Ltd	£4
Colourful Outbursts Limited	£14,395	Gospel Green Cyder Company Limited	£1
Green and Pleasant London Limited	£14,379		

This page is intentionally left blank

Age of Companies

1910-1919
H P Bulmer Limited

1930-1939
Hiram Walker (UK) Limited

1940-1949
Merrydown PLC
H.Mount & Sons Limited

1950-1959
Cornish Mead Co.Limited
Thatchers Cider Co Ltd

1960-1969
Broadland Wineries Limited
H.Weston & Sons Limited

1970-1979
Biddenden Vineyards Limited
Cornish Scrumpy Co Ltd

1980-1989
Aston Manor Limited
H & A Prestige Bottling Ltd
Marsh Barton Farm Cyder Ltd

1990-1994
Brothers Drinks Co. Limited
London Beer Co Ltd
Lyme Bay Cider Co Ltd

1995
Broughton Ales Limited

1996
Thomas Hardy Holdings Limited

1997
Heron Valley Cider Limited

1998
Thomas Hardy Burtonwood Ltd
Thomas Hardy Kendal Limited
Hartpury Heritage Trust
Whin Hill Cider Limited

1999
Branded Drinks Ltd

2000
Dunkertons Cider Co Ltd
Halewood International Limited
Legiste Limited

2001
Cornish Scrumpy Holdings Ltd

2002 [5]
Bensons Fruit Juice Limited
Cairn O'Mohr Ltd.
Orgasmic Cider Co. Ltd
Primeflow Limited
Proasset Limited

2003 [8]
Cornish Orchards Ltd
Gwatkin Cider Co. Limited
Henney's Cider Co Ltd
Hiken Limited
Lilley's Cider Limited
Ludlow Vineyard Limited
Mr. Whitehead's Cider Co Ltd
Ross-on-Wye Cider & Perry Co Ltd

2004 [5]
Armagh Cider Co Ltd
Cider Brandy Ltd
Gwynt y Ddraig Cider Ltd
Long Ashton Cider Co Ltd
Ostlers Cider Mill Limited

2005
Bygumpty Limited
Hogan's Cider Limited
Organic Country Drinks Ltd

2006
Severn Cider Ltd

2007 [5]
Analytical-Solutions UK Ltd
Broadoak Cider Co Ltd
Frampton Farm Limited
Orchard Pig Ltd
Sheppy's Cider Limited

2008
Bath Ciders Limited
Lyme Bay Winery Limited
Tutts Clump Cider Ltd

2009 [16]
Apple County Cider Co Limited
Broadlands Cider Farm Limited
Cotswold Cider Co Ltd
Damsons in Distress Limited
East Norfolk Trading Co Ltd
Gaymer Cider Co Ltd
Husthwaite Orchard Village Ltd
Kent Cider Co Ltd
Lancashire Cider Limited
Magners GB Limited
Oliver's Cider and Perry Ltd
Purbeck Cider Co Ltd
Severn Events Ltd
Wessex Cider Limited
Wessex Drinks Co Ltd
Worleys Cider Limited

January-June 2010 [7]
Bottle Kicking Cider Co Ltd
Chucklehead Cider Ltd
Handmade Cider Co Ltd
Liberty Orchards Limited
Medlar Management Limited
New Forest Cider Limited
Wibblers Brewery (Farms) Ltd

July-December 2010 [8]
Bevisol Limited
Bullington End Cider Limited
Celtic Marches Beverages Ltd
Garden Cider Co Ltd
Pips Cider Limited
Robinsons Cider Limited
Spiced Cider Co Ltd
Thistly Cross Cider Co Limited

January-June 2011
Broxbourne Brewery Ltd.
Marron (Lincoln) Ltd
Wessex Wild Plum Co Ltd

July-December 2011 [8]
Bridge Farm Cider Limited
Cidre Bouche UK Limited
Donhead Apple Co Ltd
Kingscote Winery Ltd
Lovely Cider Co Ltd
Radnage Cider Co Ltd
Scrumpy Wasp Limited
Spinney Abbey Ltd

January-March 2012 [6]
Ashover Cider Co Ltd
Dower House Cider Co Ltd.
Harry's Cider Co Ltd
Moss Cider Limited
Mr. Whitehead's Drinks Co Ltd.
Whin Hill (Norfolk) Cider Ltd

April-June 2012 [5]
Boutique Cellar Limited
Ham Hill Cider Limited
Perry's Cider Limited
St Ives Cider Limited
Wimborne Cider Co Ltd

July-September 2012 [5]
Barton Cider Co Ltd
Hawkes Cider Limited
Highworth Cider and Perry Ltd
Virtual Orchard Limited
Wise Owl Cider Ltd

October-December 2012
Appledunc Limited
Secret Orchard Cider Ltd

January-March 2013 [5]
Lambswick Drinks Co Limited
Mac Ivors Cider Co. Limited
Pearsons Ciderworks Ltd
Stockmoor Cider Limited
Toby's Cider Limited

April-June 2013 [6]
Ashridge Cider Limited
Hampshire Downs Fine Cider Co Ltd
Old Town Brewery Ltd.
Ralph's Cider Ltd
Saxby Farms Limited
Sherborne Cider Ltd

July-September 2013 [6]
Boho Cider Ltd
Cranes Drink Ltd
Dudda's Tun Ltd
Kingswood Cider Limited
Ledbury Cider and Juice Co. Ltd
North Coast Cider Co Ltd

October-December 2013 [8]
3CS Cider Limited
Barbourne Perry Limited
Chase Cider Limited
Copse House Cider Co Ltd
Cornwall Cider Co. Limited
Landshire Cider Ltd
London Cider Co Ltd
Somerset Cider Co Ltd

January-March 2014
Dee Ciders Limited
Goodness Sake Limited
Olde Mill Ltd

April-June 2014 [11]
Ashgrove Farm Produce Ltd
Essex Cider Co Ltd
Hunt's Cider Limited
Long Meadow Cider Ltd
Old Chads Orchard Ltd
Penton Park Brewery Limited
Regal Rogue Group UK Limited
Sussex South Downs Co Ltd
Tees Cider Ltd
Trinity Orchards Limited
Ty Gwyn Cider Limited

July-September 2014
Dorset Orchards Limited
Green and Pleasant London Ltd
Haygrove Evolution Limited
Highland Cider Limited

October-December 2014 [5]
Cotswold Fruit Co Ltd.
Harnser Enterprises Ltd
Mabinogion Mead Co Ltd
Orchard Origins C.I.C.
Wasted Apple Co Ltd

January 2015
Himachal Ltd
Parsonage Farm (Croscombe) Ltd

February 2015
Big Bear Cider Mill Limited
Jordan's Car Review Ltd
Mount Bank Farm Limited

March 2015
Colemans Cider Co Ltd
Conte International Limited
Hartpury Process Limited
Hoar Cross Cider Ltd

April 2015
Dampney's Remarkable Drinks Ltd.
Giggler Ltd
Honey & Daughter Limited
Meon Valley Cider Ltd

June 2015
Peak Ciders Limited

July 2015
Beard and Sabre Ltd.
Tempted Cider Co Ltd
Torre Cider Co Ltd
Umbrella Brewing Limited

August 2015
Ancient Wine and Beverages Ltd.

September 2015
Chalice Mead Limited
Chiltern Cider Co Ltd
King Offa Ltd

October 2015
Fermentorium Ltd
Iford Cider Limited

November 2015
Wild Cider Limited

December 2015
Bad Apple Cider Limited

January 2016
Revenant Cider Limited
Sandford Orchards Limited

February 2016 [5]
Creoda's Hill Ltd
Malmesbury Cider Co Ltd
Marley and Barley Ltd
Napton Cidery Limited
Tip Tap & Top Ltd

March 2016
Darley Abbey Cider Co Ltd
Pembrokeshire Cider Limited

April 2016
Bhat Ltd.
Distell International Holdings Ltd
Duxford Scrumpy Co Ltd

May 2016 [7]
Berkshire Cider Co Ltd
Crazy Dave's Cider Ltd
DJ Wines Limited
Kinross Brewery Limited
Lines Brew Co Ltd
Renegade Wines Limited
White Heron Brands Limited

June 2016
Alewife and Brewster Ltd
Apple Anarchy Limited
Pilango Limited
Viking Winery Ltd

July 2016 [6]
Apple Hoarders Limited
Harrogate Cider Co Ltd
Lyne Down Organics Limited
Samba Cidra Ltd
Showerings Cider Mill Ltd
Spryder Ltd

August 2016
Gospel Green Cyder Co Ltd
Marches Bottling and Packaging Ltd
Rutland Cider Co Ltd
Southey Brewing Co Ltd

September 2016 [5]
Angry Coot Fermentation Co Ltd.
Harleston Cider Co Ltd
Vachery Farm Cider Limited
White Rose Cider Limited
Zymurgorium Ltd

October 2016
Grumpy Frog Ltd
Lisnisky Cider Co Ltd
L. McCoy Drinks Limited
Tiddly Pommes Ltd

November 2016
Horse Kick Cider Ltd
House Brewery Limited
Thomas Paine Brewery Limited

December 2016
Halfpenny Green Cider Co Ltd
Meanwood Brewery Ltd
Salcombe Cider Co Ltd

January 2017
Ascension Cider Co. Limited
Kingston upon Hull Liqour Co Ltd
Lost Boys Brewery Ltd
Marourde Limited

February 2017
Caledonia Cider Limited
Glastonbury Drinks Co Ltd
Overtone Brewing Ltd

March 2017
Appletreewick Cider Co Ltd
Brogdale Craft Cider Limited
Woodstar Limited

April 2017 [9]
Abbiss Drinks Co Ltd
Angola Beverages Holding Co Ltd
Brute Brewing Co Ltd
Caledonian Cider Co Ltd
Colourful Outbursts Limited
Duckchicken Limited
Pomona Orchards Ltd
Spreyton Press Ltd.
Wide Eyes Enterprises Limited

May 2017 [5]
Brewers Folly Brewery Ltd.
Heaton Cider Co Ltd
Missing Link Brewing Ltd
Oast Ventures Limited
Wadys Cider Limited

June 2017
Monkey Shed Estate Brewing Co Ltd
Nightingale Cider Co Ltd
Thompstone Industries Ltd.

July 2017
Caxdon Premier Limited
Core Cider Co Ltd
Peasmarsh Cider Co Ltd

September 2017 [6]
Kendal Brewery Ltd
Kentish Maid Ltd
L'Atypique Ltd
SMSNaughton Ltd.
Sneinton Cider Co Ltd
Wye Valley Meadery Ltd

October 2017 [5]
Dean Press Cider Ltd.
Isle of Mull Winery Ltd
Loxley Cider Limited
Puxted Cider Limited
Tinston Wines & Ciders Limited

November 2017
Cooks Cider Ltd
Levscreps Ltd
Scott's Irish Whisky Ltd

December 2017 [5]
Holler Brewery Limited
Jaspels Anglesey Craft Cider Ltd
Mad Yank Brewery Ltd
Pennine Cider Limited
Turbo Cider Limited

January 2018 [6]
Bitter & Sweet UK Ltd
Broobarb Ltd
Green Shed Cider Co Ltd
Hawkins Drinks Limited
Pickers Cider Limited
Shire Meadery Ltd.

February 2018 [12]
Alejandro's Wines Limited
Bio Slim Health & Energy Drinks Ltd
Crosby Beverages Ltd
Eastern Cider House Ltd.
Islay Wines Ltd
Last Sign Brewing Co Ltd
Laughing Ass Brewery Ltd
Old Tree Brewery Ltd
One Swan Ltd
Saint Patricks Ltd
Simply Cider Ltd
Ten Tors Brewery Ltd

March 2018 [7]
AB Vaults Group Limited
Grumpy Wasp Ltd
Lamson Wine Co Ltd
Luminati Wine Limited
Neptune SA Ltd
Noahs Estate Ltd
Wasted Opportunity Limited

April 2018 [6]
Crossroads Brewery Limited
Farcial Ltd
Festival Beverage and Property Services
Infirock Ltd
James Lewis Cider Ltd
Little Wolf Brewing Limited

May 2018 [9]
BF Wines UK Ltd
Bockleton Court Limited
Diamations Ltd
East Coast Cider Co Ltd
Embev Ltd
Halorank Ltd
Malton Cider Ltd
Onefolks Ltd
Solway Spirits Ltd

June 2018 [11]
AA & D Limited
Alcohol Beverages Co Ltd
Brewbarb Ltd
Cool Brew Dept Ltd
Covenflare Ltd
Drapex Ltd
Evopan Ltd
Fruito Soft Drinks Limited
Incubuzz Ltd
Shrewsbury Cider Co Ltd
Starshade Ltd

July 2018 [8]
Calmcorn Ltd
Craftwater Brewing Co Ltd
Ginomine Ltd
Green Valley Cyder Limited
Manmax Ltd
Noddy's Cider Ltd
Portsmouth Distillery Co Ltd
Rock Hill Cider Co Ltd

August 2018 [5]
Polaners Ltd
Sephylia Ltd
Silverpelt Ltd
Still Wild Limited
Tripper Cider Ltd

September 2018 [11]
Adhinton Ltd
Aohimetron Ltd
Arkustemple Ltd
Crai Cider Co Ltd
Isle of Islay Cider Co Ltd
Little Teapot Ltd
Not Real Wine Co Ltd
Sibling Winery Limited
Simoncraft Limited
Sky Pirate Ltd
TCC (Assets) Ltd

October 2018 [9]
Caneys Cider Ltd
Cider Mill Limited
Dunwrights Cider Co Ltd
Gentleman's Cider Ltd.
Ginsecco Ltd
Jars Cider Ltd
Medland Manor Vineyard Ltd.
Polecat Cider Limited
South Downs Cider Limited

November 2018
Laycock Cider Ltd
Polgoon Vineyard Ltd
Sadler-Wilson & Read Ltd
Westmoor Botanicals Limited

December 2018
Clandestine Distillery Limited
Twin Barrel Brewery Limited

January 2019 [9]
A Little Luxury Distillery Ltd
Batch Cider Ltd
Bobo Roots Wine Ltd
Flower Miners Limited
Hidden Orchard Ltd
New Union Brewing Co Ltd
Sharpham Wine Limited
Tremayne Food and Drink Ltd
W & W Drinks Ltd

February 2019 [8]
Black Dog Meadery Ltd
Bumble Mead Ltd
Cheltenham Cider Co Ltd
Craft Cider Limited
Nada General Trading Ltd
Somerset Cider Solutions Ltd
Symons Cyder & Fruit Wine Co Ltd
Wild Life Botanicals Ltd

Geographic Distribution by County

Co Antrim
Tempted Cider Co Ltd

Co Armagh [5]
Armagh Cider Co Ltd
Lisnisky Cider Co Ltd
Long Meadow Cider Ltd
Mac Ivors Cider Co. Limited
Toby's Cider Limited

Co Down
Brute Brewing Co Ltd
Pomona Orchards Ltd

Co Fermanagh
Scott's Irish Whisky Ltd

Co Londonderry
One Swan Ltd

Aberdeenshire
Brewbarb Ltd
Broobarb Ltd

Angus
Caledonia Cider Limited

Argyll
Isle of Islay Cider Co Ltd

Dumfries & Galloway
Solway Spirits Ltd

Highland
Caledonian Cider Co Ltd

Isle of Mull
Isle of Mull Winery Ltd

Kinross-shire
Kinross Brewery Limited

Lanarkshire
Broughton Ales Limited
Ginsecco Ltd
Overtone Brewing Ltd

Perthshire
Cairn O'Mohr Ltd.

Ross-shire
Highland Cider Limited

Anglesey
Jaspels Anglesey Craft Cider Ltd

Avon
Thatchers Cider Co Ltd

Bedfordshire
Samba Cidra Ltd

Berkshire [9]
Apple County Cider Co Limited
Berkshire Cider Co Ltd
Crazy Dave's Cider Ltd
Green Shed Cider Co Ltd
Jars Cider Ltd
Polecat Cider Limited
Simoncraft Limited
Tutts Clump Cider Ltd
W & W Drinks Ltd

Buckinghamshire
Bullington End Cider Limited
Chiltern Cider Co Ltd
Radnage Cider Co Ltd

Cambridgeshire [5]
Duxford Scrumpy Co Ltd
Green and Pleasant London Ltd
Saxby Farms Limited
Spinney Abbey Ltd
Trinity Orchards Limited

Cardiganshire
Black Dog Meadery Ltd
Shire Meadery Ltd.

Cheshire [6]
Alejandro's Wines Limited
Thomas Hardy Burtonwood Ltd
Thomas Hardy Holdings Limited
Thomas Hardy Kendal Limited
Luminati Wine Limited
Old Chads Orchard Ltd

Cornwall [10]
Bath Ciders Limited
Cornish Mead Co.Limited
Cornwall Cider Co. Limited
Flower Miners Limited
Hidden Orchard Ltd
North Coast Cider Co Ltd
Polgoon Vineyard Ltd
St Ives Cider Limited
Tremayne Food and Drink Ltd
Wasted Apple Co Ltd

Cumbria
Kendal Brewery Ltd
New Union Brewing Co Ltd

Derbyshire
Ashover Cider Co Ltd
Darley Abbey Cider Co Ltd
Not Real Wine Co Ltd

Devon [23]
Ashridge Cider Limited
Cider Brandy Ltd
Cornish Scrumpy Co Ltd
Cornish Scrumpy Holdings Ltd
Craftwater Brewing Co Ltd
Gaymer Cider Co Ltd
Green Valley Cyder Limited
Heron Valley Cider Limited
Honey & Daughter Limited
House Brewery Limited
Hunt's Cider Limited
London Cider Co Ltd
Lyme Bay Cider Co Ltd
Lyme Bay Winery Limited
Magners GB Limited
Marsh Barton Farm Cyder Ltd
Medland Manor Vineyard Ltd.
Ostlers Cider Mill Limited
Salcombe Cider Co Ltd
Sandford Orchards Limited
Sharpham Wine Limited
Spreyton Press Ltd.
Thompstone Industries Ltd.

Dorset [12]
Brewers Folly Brewery Ltd.
Cidre Bouche UK Limited
Copse House Cider Co Ltd
Donhead Apple Co Ltd
Dorset Orchards Limited
Harry's Cider Co Ltd
Landshire Cider Ltd
Laycock Cider Ltd
Liberty Orchards Limited
Noddy's Cider Ltd
Sherborne Cider Ltd
Wimborne Cider Co Ltd

Essex [8]
Apple Anarchy Limited
Big Bear Cider Mill Limited
Broxbourne Brewery Ltd.
Conte International Limited
Essex Cider Co Ltd
London Beer Co Ltd
Neptune SA Ltd
Wibblers Brewery (Farms) Ltd

Flintshire
Dee Ciders Limited

Gloucestershire [17]
Abbiss Drinks Co Ltd
Beard and Sabre Ltd.
Bensons Fruit Juice Limited
Branded Drinks Ltd
Cheltenham Cider Co Ltd
Cotswold Fruit Co Ltd.
Craft Cider Limited
Dower House Cider Co. Ltd.
Dunkertons Cider Co Ltd
Hartpury Heritage Trust
Hartpury Process Limited
Jordan's Car Review Ltd
Merrydown PLC
Pearsons Ciderworks Ltd
Severn Cider Ltd
Severn Events Ltd
Wild Cider Limited

Hampshire [11]
Dampney's Remarkable Drinks Ltd.
Hampshire Downs Fine Cider Co Ltd
Meon Valley Cider Ltd
Mr. Whitehead's Cider Co Ltd
Mr. Whitehead's Drinks Co Ltd.
New Forest Cider Limited
Penton Park Brewery Limited
Portsmouth Distillery Co Ltd
Purbeck Cider Co Ltd
Silverpelt Ltd
Wessex Wild Plum Co Ltd

Herefordshire [18]
Bevisol Limited
Gwatkin Cider Co. Limited
Haygrove Evolution Limited
Henney's Cider Co Ltd
King Offa Ltd
Ledbury Cider and Juice Co. Ltd
Lyne Down Organics Limited
Oliver's Cider and Perry Ltd
Orchard Origins C.I.C.
Orgasmic Cider Co. Ltd
Pips Cider Limited
Primeflow Limited
Ross-on-Wye Cider & Perry Co Ltd
Stockmoor Cider Limited
Ty Gwyn Cider Limited
H.Weston & Sons Limited
White Heron Brands Limited
Wide Eyes Enterprises Limited

Hertfordshire [6]
Analytical-Solutions UK Ltd
Cranes Drink Ltd
Lancashire Cider Limited
Lost Boys Brewery Ltd
Southey Brewing Co Ltd
Spryder Ltd

Kent [17]
Alewife and Brewster Ltd
Biddenden Vineyards Limited
Brogdale Craft Cider Limited
Dudda's Tun Ltd
Kent Cider Co Ltd
Kentish Maid Ltd
Kingswood Cider Limited
Marourde Limited
L. McCoy Drinks Limited
H.Mount & Sons Limited
Nightingale Cider Co Ltd
Oast Ventures Limited
Organic Country Drinks Ltd
Puxted Cider Limited
SMSNaughton Ltd.
Spiced Cider Co Ltd
Wise Owl Cider Ltd

Lancashire [16]
Calmcorn Ltd
Diamations Ltd
Drapex Ltd
Farcial Ltd
H & A Prestige Bottling Ltd
Halorank Ltd
Infirock Ltd
Legiste Limited
Little Teapot Ltd
Manmax Ltd
Onefolks Ltd
Polaners Ltd
Proasset Limited
Sephylia Ltd
Starshade Ltd
Zymurgorium Ltd

Leicestershire
Bottle Kicking Cider Co Ltd
Cooks Cider Ltd
Rutland Cider Co Ltd
Simply Cider Ltd

Lincolnshire
Damsons in Distress Limited
Marron (Lincoln) Ltd
Thomas Paine Brewery Limited
Tip Tap & Top Ltd

London [39]
A Little Luxury Distillery Ltd
AB Vaults Group Limited
Alcohol Beverages Co Ltd
Angry Coot Fermentation Co Ltd.
BF Wines UK Ltd
Batch Cider Ltd
Bitter & Sweet UK Ltd
Bobo Roots Wine Ltd
H P Bulmer Limited
Caxdon Premier Limited
Cider Mill Limited
Cornish Orchards Ltd
Crosby Beverages Ltd
Duckchicken Limited
Eastern Cider House Ltd.
Embev Ltd
Fermentorium Ltd
Frampton Farm Limited
Fruito Soft Drinks Limited
Gentleman's Cider Ltd.
Giggler Ltd
Hawkes Cider Limited
Islay Wines Ltd
L'Atypique Ltd
Levscreps Ltd
Nada General Trading Ltd
Pilango Limited
Renegade Wines Limited
Revenant Cider Limited
Rock Hill Cider Co Ltd
Saint Patricks Ltd
Sky Pirate Ltd
TCC (Assets) Ltd
Ten Tors Brewery Ltd
Tripper Cider Ltd
Umbrella Brewing Limited
Hiram Walker (UK) Limited
Wasted Opportunity Limited
Wild Life Botanicals Ltd

Merseyside
Halewood International Limited
Moss Cider Limited

Middlesex
Mad Yank Brewery Ltd
Woodstar Limited

Midlothian [5]
AA & D Limited
Ancient Wine and Beverages Ltd.
Festival Beverage and Property Services
Little Wolf Brewing Limited
Thistly Cross Cider Co Limited

Monmouthshire [7]
Boutique Cellar Limited
Bygumpty Limited
Clandestine Distillery Limited
Gospel Green Cyder Co Ltd
Lines Brew Co Ltd
Mabinogion Mead Co Ltd
Wye Valley Meadery Ltd

Norfolk [7]
Broadland Wineries Limited
Dean Press Cider Ltd.
East Norfolk Trading Co Ltd
Harleston Cider Co Ltd
Hiken Limited
Whin Hill (Norfolk) Cider Ltd
Whin Hill Cider Limited

Northamptonshire
Ginomine Ltd
Virtual Orchard Limited

Nottinghamshire [5]
Bad Apple Cider Limited
Grumpy Wasp Ltd
Loxley Cider Limited
Scrumpy Wasp Limited
Sneinton Cider Co Ltd

Oxfordshire [5]
3CS Cider Limited
Barton Cider Co Ltd
Colourful Outbursts Limited
Creoda's Hill Ltd
Tiddly Pommes Ltd

Pembrokeshire
Pembrokeshire Cider Limited
Still Wild Limited

Powys
Crai Cider Co Ltd
Ralph's Cider Ltd

Rhondda Cynon Taf
Gwynt y Ddraig Cider Ltd

Shropshire
Ludlow Vineyard Limited
Robinsons Cider Limited
Shrewsbury Cider Co Ltd

Somerset [25]
Appledunc Limited
Ashgrove Farm Produce Ltd
Bhat Ltd.
Bridge Farm Cider Limited
Broadlands Cider Farm Limited
Broadoak Cider Co Ltd
Brothers Drinks Co. Limited
Glastonbury Drinks Co Ltd
Ham Hill Cider Limited
Lilley's Cider Limited
Long Ashton Cider Co Ltd
Olde Mill Ltd
Orchard Pig Ltd
Parsonage Farm (Croscombe) Ltd
Perry's Cider Limited
Secret Orchard Cider Ltd
Sheppy's Cider Limited
Showerings Cider Mill Ltd
Somerset Cider Co Ltd
Somerset Cider Solutions Ltd
Torre Cider Co Ltd
Twin Barrel Brewery Limited
Viking Winery Ltd
Wadys Cider Limited
Worleys Cider Limited

Staffordshire [7]
Chase Cider Limited
Halfpenny Green Cider Co Ltd
Hawkins Drinks Limited
Hoar Cross Cider Ltd
Lovely Cider Co Ltd
Peak Ciders Limited
Symons Cyder & Fruit Wine Co Ltd

Suffolk
Core Cider Co Ltd
DJ Wines Limited
Harnser Enterprises Ltd
Last Sign Brewing Co Ltd

Surrey [7]
Angola Beverages Holding Co Ltd
Apple Hoarders Limited
Chalice Mead Limited

Distell International Holdings Ltd
Garden Cider Co Ltd
Horse Kick Cider Ltd
Vachery Farm Cider Limited

Sussex [14]
Ascension Cider Co. Limited
Chucklehead Cider Ltd
Goodness Sake Limited
Holler Brewery Limited
Kingscote Winery Ltd
Marley and Barley Ltd
Missing Link Brewing Ltd
Old Tree Brewery Ltd
Peasmarsh Cider Co Ltd
Pickers Cider Limited
Regal Rogue Group UK Limited
South Downs Cider Limited
Sussex South Downs Co Ltd
Tinston Wines & Ciders Limited

Tyne & Wear
Crossroads Brewery Limited
East Coast Cider Co Ltd
Heaton Cider Co Ltd

Warwickshire [5]
Caneys Cider Ltd
Grumpy Frog Ltd
Hogan's Cider Limited
Napton Cidery Limited
Sibling Winery Limited

West Midlands
Adhinton Ltd
Aohimetron Ltd
Arkustemple Ltd
Aston Manor Limited

Wiltshire [10]
Boho Cider Ltd
Bumble Mead Ltd
Cotswold Cider Co Ltd
Handmade Cider Co Ltd
Highworth Cider and Perry Ltd
Iford Cider Limited
Malmesbury Cider Co Ltd
Old Town Brewery Ltd.
Wessex Cider Limited
Wessex Drinks Co Ltd

Worcestershire [6]
Barbourne Perry Limited
Bockleton Court Limited
Celtic Marches Beverages Ltd
Lambswick Drinks Co Limited
Marches Bottling and Packaging Ltd
Monkey Shed Estate Brewing Co Ltd

Yorkshire [26]
Appletreewick Cider Co Ltd
Bio Slim Health & Energy Drinks Ltd
Colemans Cider Co Ltd
Cool Brew Dept Ltd
Covenflare Ltd
Dunwrights Cider Co Ltd
Evopan Ltd
Harrogate Cider Co Ltd
Himachal Ltd
Husthwaite Orchard Village Ltd
Incubuzz Ltd
Kingston upon Hull Liqour Co Ltd
Lamson Wine Co Ltd
Laughing Ass Brewery Ltd
James Lewis Cider Ltd
Malton Cider Ltd
Meanwood Brewery Ltd
Medlar Management Limited
Mount Bank Farm Limited
Noahs Estate Ltd
Pennine Cider Limited
Sadler-Wilson & Read Ltd
Tees Cider Ltd
Turbo Cider Limited
Westmoor Botanicals Limited
White Rose Cider Limited

Company Profiles

3CS Cider Limited
Incorporated: 21 November 2013 *Employees:* 1
Net Worth Deficit: £41,700 *Total Assets:* £12,645
Registered Office: Units 4 & 5 Swinford Farm, Eynsham, Oxford, OX29 4BL
Shareholders: Jasper Rory Barrington Galloway; Toby Grafftey-Smith; William Ronald Sacheverell Sitwell
Officers: James Alexander Stephen Buchan [1964] Director/Investor; Jasper Rory Barrington Galloway [1971] Director/Designer; William Ronald Sacheverell Sitwell [1969] Director/Writer, Editor and Broadcaster

A Little Luxury Distillery Ltd
Incorporated: 23 January 2019
Registered Office: 20-22 Wenlock Road, London, N1 7GU
Shareholders: Barbara Ann Daughtrey; Laura Elizabeth Daughtrey
Officers: Barbara Ann Daughtrey, Secretary; Barbara Ann Daughtrey [1953] Director; Laura Elizabeth Daughtrey [1981] Director

AA & D Limited
Incorporated: 6 June 2018
Registered Office: 19a Hill Street, Edinburgh, EH2 3JP
Shareholders: Angus Kennedy Morrison; Andrew James Husband; Dougal Gunn Sharp
Officers: Iain Sydney Russell Baird, Secretary; Andrew James Husband [1967] Director; Angus Kennedy Morrison [1961] Director; Dougal Gunn Sharp [1972] Director

AB Vaults Group Limited
Incorporated: 8 March 2018
Registered Office: 5 Academy House, 1 Thunderer Street, London, E13 9DP
Major Shareholder: Samuel Ndungu
Officers: Samuel N K Banks [1988] Director/Entrepreneur [Kenyan]

Abbiss Drinks Company Limited
Incorporated: 7 April 2017
Net Worth Deficit: £2,673 *Total Assets:* £95,053
Registered Office: Royal Mews, St Georges Place, Cheltenham, Glos, GL50 3PQ
Shareholders: Simon Timothy Abbiss; Karen Sarah Abbiss
Officers: Karen Sarah Abbiss, Secretary; Karen Sarah Abbiss [1964] Director; Simon Timothy Abbiss [1961] Director

Adhinton Ltd
Incorporated: 26 September 2018
Registered Office: Suite 4, 43 Hagley Road, Stourbridge, W Midlands, DY8 1QR
Major Shareholder: Rhys Bennett
Officers: Rhiena Ramirez [1995] Director [Filipino]

Alcohol Beverages Company Ltd
Incorporated: 15 June 2018
Registered Office: Pitts and Seeus, Omnibus Business Centre, 39-41 North Road, London, N7 9DP
Major Shareholder: James Gerald McMackin
Officers: James Generald McMackin [1961] Director [Irish]

Alejandro's Wines Limited
Incorporated: 7 February 2018
Registered Office: Riverside House, Kings Reach Business Park, Yew Street, Stockport, Cheshire, SK4 2HD
Major Shareholder: Alejandro Marzana Hawrylak
Officers: Alejandro Marzana Hawrylak [1978] Director [Spanish]

Alewife and Brewster Ltd
Incorporated: 24 June 2016
Registered Office: 37 High Steet, Wingham, Canterbury, Kent, CT3 1AB
Shareholders: Peter Robert May; Louise Anne May
Officers: Peter Robert May, Secretary; Louise Anne May [1962] Director/Psychotherapist; Peter Robert May [1963] Director/Business Development Executive

Analytical-Solutions UK Ltd
Incorporated: 20 March 2007
Net Worth: £14,452 *Total Assets:* £27,473
Registered Office: 106 Woodland Drive, St Albans, Herts, AL4 0ET
Major Shareholder: Yde Bouke Yntema
Officers: Anne Claire Bordier, Secretary; Yde Bouke Yntema [1969] Director/Analyst [Dutch]

Ancient Wine and Beverages Ltd.
Incorporated: 13 August 2015
Registered Office: 4th Floor, 115 George Street, Edinburgh, EH2 4JN
Shareholders: Garreth Samuel Roberts; Mark Rutter
Officers: Garreth Samuel Roberts [1967] Director/Freelance Designer & Researcher; Mark Christian Rutter [1980] Director

Angola Beverages Holding Company Limited
Incorporated: 12 April 2017
Registered Office: Avalon House, 72 Lower Mortlake Road, Richmond, Surrey, TW9 2JY
Parent: Distell International Holdings Limited
Officers: Karen Spy, Secretary; Werner Nolte [1976] Director/Head of Finance [South African]

Angry Coot Fermentation Company Ltd.
Incorporated: 22 September 2016
Registered Office: Flat 35, Tequila Wharf, 681 Commercial Road, London, E14 7LG
Major Shareholder: Samuel Fraser Thomas
Officers: Samuel Fraser Thomas [1990] Director/Brewer

Aohimetron Ltd
Incorporated: 11 September 2018
Registered Office: Suite 4, 43 Hagley Road, Stourbridge, W Midlands, DY8 1QR
Major Shareholder: Sheridan Greenwood
Officers: Carla Tizon [1995] Director [Filipino]

Apple Anarchy Limited
Incorporated: 6 June 2016
Net Worth Deficit: £179
Registered Office: 28 Usk Road, Aveley, South Ockendon, Essex, RM15 4PB
Officers: Richard James Venour [1980] Director/Brewer

Apple County Cider Co Limited
Incorporated: 1 April 2009
Net Worth: £17,994 *Total Assets:* £104,675
Registered Office: Clere House, West Street, Burghclere, Newbury, Berks, RG20 9LB
Major Shareholder: Benedict Alan Culpin
Officers: Sophie Louisa Dorothea Neill, Secretary; Benedict Alan Culpin [1973] Production and Sales Director; Stephanie Adele Acton Culpin [1977] Marketing Director

Apple Hoarders Limited
Incorporated: 27 July 2016
Net Worth: £3,176 *Total Assets:* £3,176
Registered Office: 1 Dancer Road, Richmond, Surrey, TW9 4LD
Shareholders: Jamie Simon Oldroyd; Nicholas William Horan; Alisdair James Willett
Officers: Nicholas William Horan [1986] Director/Global Design Associate; Jamie Simon Oldroyd [1986] Director/Business Change Manager; Alisdair James Willett [1987] Director/Mechanical Project Manager

Appledunc Limited
Incorporated: 15 October 2012
Registered Office: Manor Farm, Brinsea Lane, Congresbury, Somerset, BS49 5JN
Shareholder: Elsie Bowen
Officers: Elsie Bowen, Secretary; Elsie Bowen [1930] Director; Angus Peter Michael Leather [1996] Director/Student; Emily Laura Jane Leather [1994] Director/Student

The Appletreewick Cider Company Ltd
Incorporated: 20 March 2017
Registered Office: 2 Fell View, Appletreewick, Skipton, N Yorks, BD23 6DB
Shareholders: Alastair Allen; Adam Mason
Officers: Alastair Allen [1980] Director/Cider Maker; Adam Mason [1980] Director/Cider Maker

Arkustemple Ltd
Incorporated: 13 September 2018
Registered Office: Suite 4, 43 Hagley Road, Stourbridge, W Midlands, DY8 1QR
Major Shareholder: Jade McDermott
Officers: Mary Elaine Bonan [1994] Director [Filipino]

Armagh Cider Company Ltd
Incorporated: 8 December 2004
Net Worth: £107,685 *Total Assets:* £608,039
Registered Office: 76-78 Church Street, Portadown, Co Armagh, BT62 7EU
Officers: Kelly Elizabeth Crawford, Secretary; Kelly Elizabeth Crawford [1981] Director; Helen Elizabeth Troughton [1954] Director; Mark Troughton [1983] Director; Philip Samuel Troughton [1953] Director

Ascension Cider Co. Limited
Incorporated: 4 January 2017
Net Worth: £2,919 *Total Assets:* £41,539
Registered Office: York House, The Stud Farm Stables, Gainsborough Lane, Polegate, E Sussex, BN26 5HQ
Major Shareholder: Martyn John Billing
Officers: Martyn John Billing [1961] Director/Marketing Consultancy; Matthew David Anthony Billing [1991] Director/Cider Maker

Ashgrove Farm Produce Ltd
Incorporated: 22 April 2014 *Employees:* 1
Net Worth: £1,237 *Total Assets:* £25,710
Registered Office: Ashgrove Farm, Sand, Wedmore, Somerset, BS28 4XF
Shareholders: Toby John Lee; Anna Lena Lee
Officers: Anna Lena Lee [1976] Director [Swedish]

Ashover Cider Company Limited
Incorporated: 18 January 2012
Net Worth: £6,221 *Total Assets:* £60,520
Registered Office: The Wheatcroft, Butts Road, Chesterfield, Derbys, S45 0AX
Shareholders: Michael Philbin; Michelle Rafter
Officers: Michael Philbin [1959] Director/Consultant; Michelle Rafter [1981] Director/Assistant Premises Manager

Ashridge Cider Limited
Incorporated: 2 April 2013
Net Worth Deficit: £5,175 *Total Assets:* £458,463
Registered Office: Barkingdon Farm, Staverton, Totnes, Devon, TQ9 6AN
Major Shareholder: Jason Mitchell
Officers: Jason Mitchell [1952] Director

Aston Manor Limited
Incorporated: 15 February 1983 *Employees:* 299
Previous: Aston Manor Brewery Company Limited
Net Worth: £28,624,414 *Total Assets:* £55,704,092
Registered Office: Deykin Avenue, Birmingham, B6 7BH
Officers: James Douglas Ellis, Secretary; James Douglas Ellis [1978] Director; Yves Jacobs [1963] Director [French]; Gordon Paul Hazell Johncox [1961] Managing Director; Marc Roubaud [1958] Director/General Manager [French]; Ludovic Spiers [1960] Director [French]

Bad Apple Cider Limited
Incorporated: 29 December 2015
Registered Office: Rosedean Farm, Mark Lane, East Markhan, Newark, Notts, NG22 0QU
Major Shareholder: Timothy Paul Needham
Officers: Timothy Paul Needham, Secretary; Timothy Paul Needham [1960] Director/Brewer

Barbourne Perry Limited
Incorporated: 1 October 2013
Registered Office: 19 York Place, Worcester, WR1 3DR
Major Shareholder: Richard David Leonard Reynolds
Officers: Richard David Leonard Reynolds [1969] Director/Cider Maker; Suzanne Ginevera Reynolds [1974] Director/Cider Maker

Barton Cider Company Limited
Incorporated: 26 July 2012
Registered Office: 30 Bankside Court, Stationfields, Kidlington, Oxon, OX5 1JE
Officers: Dr Carol Janet Lister, Secretary; Dr Kevin Paul Isaac [1958] Director/Geologist

Batch Cider Ltd
Incorporated: 30 January 2019
Registered Office: 12 Greenway, London, N14 6NN
Major Shareholder: Carl Reid
Officers: Carl Reid [1993] Director/Architect

Bath Ciders Limited
Incorporated: 28 July 2008
Registered Office: 63 Trevarthian Road, St Austell, Cornwall, PL25 4BY
Parent: St Austell Brewery Company Limited
Officers: Colin John Stratton, Secretary; Thomas Adam Luck [1956] Director; Simon James Staughton [1959] Director

Beard and Sabre Ltd.
Incorporated: 20 July 2015
Net Worth Deficit: £27,502 *Total Assets:* £17,685
Registered Office: Beard and Sabre, Unit 2b Norcote Workshops, Norcote, Cirencester, Glos, GL7 5RH
Major Shareholder: Thomas James William Dunn
Officers: Thomas James William Dunn [1992] Director

Bensons Fruit Juice Limited
Incorporated: 21 August 2002 *Employees:* 15
Net Worth: £128,992 *Total Assets:* £590,317
Registered Office: Sandyhill Farm, Sherborne, Glos, GL54 3DS
Shareholders: Alexia Louise Benson; Jeremy Benson
Officers: Alexia Benson, Secretary; Alexia Louise Benson [1973] Director; Jeremy Benson [1971] Director

The Berkshire Cider Company Ltd
Incorporated: 26 May 2016
Registered Office: 6 Altmore, Cherry Garden Lane, Maidenhead, Berks, SL6 3QG
Major Shareholder: David Philip Snowden
Officers: David Philip Snowden [1970] Director/Cider Maker

Bevisol Limited
Incorporated: 19 October 2010 *Employees:* 46
Net Worth: £6,514,006 *Total Assets:* £13,857,646
Registered Office: Unit 1a Orchard Business Park, Bromyard Road, Ledbury, Herefords, HR8 1LG
Parent: Dohler Group SE
Officers: Lisa Annabel Newall, Secretary; Simon Rayland Hewitt Fletcher [1970] Commercial Director; Frank Karl-Heinz Lindenberg [1964] Director/Graduate Brewermaster [German]; Christopher James Howard Newall [1963] Director; Martin Walsh [1951] Director

BF Wines UK Ltd
Incorporated: 17 May 2018
Registered Office: Kemp House, 160 City Road, London, EC1V 2NX
Officers: Dr Olufolake Akinduro-Aje, Secretary; Benson Aje [1972] Director/Criminologist

Bhat Ltd.
Incorporated: 25 April 2016
Registered Office: Box Cottage, 33 High Street, Yatton, Bristol, BS49 4JD
Officers: Daniel Arthur [1983] Director/Cider Producer; Gary Byrom [1967] Director/Cider Producer; Richard Thomas [1965] Director/Cider Producer

Biddenden Vineyards Limited
Incorporated: 3 March 1975 *Employees:* 20
Net Worth: £112,681 *Total Assets:* £830,730
Registered Office: Little Whatmans Farm, Biddenden, Kent, TN27 8DF
Shareholder: Richard Julian Barnes
Officers: Sally Barnes, Secretary; Richard Julian Barnes [1960] Managing Director; Sally Barnes [1961] Director/Company Secretary

The Big Bear Cider Mill Limited
Incorporated: 18 February 2015 *Employees:* 1
Previous: The Big Bear Brewery Ltd
Net Worth Deficit: £917 *Total Assets:* £702
Registered Office: The Barn, Tumblers Green, Braintree, Essex, CM77 8AZ
Officers: Emily Alice Butler [1990] Director; Kathryn Ella Hughes [1963] Director; William Michael Hughes [1993] Director

Bio Slim Health & Energy Drinks Limited
Incorporated: 28 February 2018
Registered Office: Bridge House, 64-72 Mabgate, Leeds, LS9 7DZ
Major Shareholder: Robert (Elias) Wilson
Officers: Robert Wilson [1941] Director (CEO)

Bitter & Sweet UK Ltd
Incorporated: 10 January 2018
Registered Office: Flat 1, 40 Barretts Grove, London, N16 8AJ
Major Shareholder: Benjamin de Vos
Officers: Benjamin de Vos [1977] Managing Director

Black Dog Meadery Ltd
Incorporated: 13 February 2019
Registered Office: New Quay Honey Farm, Cross Inn, Cardigan, Llandysul, Ceredigion, SA44 6NN
Shareholder: Samuel Charles Orlando Cooper
Officers: Samuel Charles Orlando Cooper, Secretary; Samuel Charles Orlando Cooper [1975] Director; Margaret Woodcock [1980] Director

Bobo Roots Wine Ltd
Incorporated: 14 January 2019
Registered Office: 62 Dixon Road, South Norwood, London, SE25 6UE
Major Shareholder: Beauce Lyvio Audrey
Officers: Beauce Lyvio Audrey [1983] Director/Electrician [French]

Bockleton Court Limited
Incorporated: 22 May 2018
Registered Office: Bockleton Court, Bockleton, Tenbury Wells, Worcs, WR15 8PP
Shareholder: Paul John Garrod
Officers: Paul John Garrod [1946] Director

Boho Cider Ltd
Incorporated: 16 July 2013
Registered Office: 54 Coleshill, Swindon, Wilts, SN6 7PT
Major Shareholder: Rory Julian Souter
Officers: Rory Julian Souter [1967] Managing Director

The Bottle Kicking Cider Company Limited
Incorporated: 11 January 2010
Net Worth Deficit: £43,864 *Total Assets:* £40,824
Registered Office: Cross Farm, 4 The Cross, Hallaton, Market Harborough, Leics, LE16 8UA
Shareholder: Robert Everett Morton
Officers: Tracey Morton, Secretary; Robert Everett Morton [1961] Director; Tracey Joanne Morton [1964] Director

The Boutique Cellar Limited
Incorporated: 7 June 2012
Net Worth Deficit: £30,394 *Total Assets:* £128,656
Registered Office: Low Barn, Gwehelog, Usk, Monmouthshire, NP15 1HY
Officers: Sarah Thompson [1976] Director

Branded Drinks Ltd
Incorporated: 16 September 1999 *Employees:* 24
Net Worth: £1,041,037 *Total Assets:* £3,886,575
Registered Office: The Bottling Works, Unit 1 The Business Park, Tufthorn Avenue, Coleford, Glos, GL16 8PN
Major Shareholder: Jonathan Charles Calver
Officers: Gray Bensted Olliver, Secretary; Jonathan Charles Calver [1970] Managing Director; Gray Bensted Olliver [1949] Sales & Marketing Director

Brewbarb Ltd
Incorporated: 22 June 2018
Registered Office: 34 Balgownie Court, Aberdeen, AB24 1XF
Major Shareholder: Christopher Ian Henderson
Officers: Christopher Ian Henderson [1976] Director/ROV Pilot

Brewers Folly Brewery Ltd.
Incorporated: 12 May 2017
Net Worth: £506 *Total Assets:* £593
Registered Office: Ashton Farm House, Stanbridge, Wimborne, Dorset, BH21 4JD
Officers: Richard Rufus Francis Glyn [1971] Director/Charity Trustee; Dean Patrick Harris [1988] Director/Mechanic; Eric Frank Nelson [1968] Director/IT Consultant [American]

Bridge Farm Cider Limited
Incorporated: 3 October 2011
Net Worth: £59,896 *Total Assets:* £186,605
Registered Office: East Chinnock, Yeovil, Somerset, BA22 9EA
Shareholders: Nigel Ian Stewart; Fina Stewart
Officers: Fina Stewart [1960] Director/Administration Assistant; Nigel Ian Stewart [1961] Director/Cider Maker

Broadland Wineries Limited
Incorporated: 15 September 1965 *Employees:* 135
Net Worth: £7,524,194 *Total Assets:* £24,202,070
Registered Office: Chapel Street, Cawston, Norwich, NR10 4BG
Parent: Arrhenius Holdings Ltd
Officers: Robert Bell [1979] Director/Chartered Accountant; Hew Richard Hamilton Dalrymple BT [1955] Director; Jonathon Mark Lansley [1962] Director/Chairman

Broadlands Cider Farm Limited
Incorporated: 4 March 2009
Net Worth Deficit: £17,521 *Total Assets:* £14,458
Registered Office: Orchard Fields, Claverton, Bath, BA2 7BB
Major Shareholder: Richard Selby Hudson
Officers: Richard Selby Hudson [1966] Director/Cider Marketing & Retailing

Broadoak Cider Company Limited
Incorporated: 24 April 2007
Net Worth Deficit: £53,458 *Total Assets:* £457,775
Registered Office: Scott Cottage, Pagans Hill, Chew Stoke, Bristol, BS40 8UQ
Major Shareholder: Nina Maria Emily Brunt
Officers: Nina Maria Emily Brunt, Secretary; Nina Maria Emily Brunt [1950] Director; Steven Lee Brunt [1979] Director

Brogdale Craft Cider Limited
Incorporated: 31 March 2017 *Employees:* 2
Net Worth Deficit: £7,982 *Total Assets:* £92,114
Registered Office: Aranda, Station Road, Eynsford, Dartford, Kent, DA4 0EJ
Major Shareholder: John Lewington
Officers: John Lewington [1970] Director

Broobarb Ltd
Incorporated: 26 January 2018
Registered Office: 34 Balgownie Court, Aberdeen, AB24 1XF
Major Shareholder: Christopher Ian Henderson
Officers: Jane Henderson, Secretary; Christopher Ian Henderson [1976] Director

Brothers Drinks Co. Limited
Incorporated: 30 April 1992 *Employees:* 185
Net Worth: £56,965,680 *Total Assets:* £72,885,224
Registered Office: 4th Floor, St Catherines Court, Berkeley Place, Clifton, Bristol, BS8 1BQ
Officers: Iain David Glen, Secretary; Christopher John Courage [1962] Director; Iain David Glen [1969] Director/Accountant; Jonathan Showering [1962] Director/Financial Advisor; Matthew Herbert Showering [1964] Director/Marketing Advisor

Broughton Ales Limited
Incorporated: 14 August 1995 *Employees:* 9
Net Worth: £269,366 *Total Assets:* £502,688
Registered Office: Main Street, Broughton Village, Biggar, S Lanarks, ML12 6HQ
Shareholders: Stephen Lawrence McCarney; David Andrew McGowan; John Simon Hunt
Officers: John Simon Hunt [1963] Director; Stephen Lawrence McCarney [1961] Director; David Andrew McGowan [1963] Director

Broxbourne Brewery Ltd.
Incorporated: 18 May 2011 *Employees:* 2
Previous: Chameleon By Design Ltd
Net Worth Deficit: £38,642 *Total Assets:* £44,894
Registered Office: 6 St Marys Mead, Broomfield, Chelmsford, Essex, CM1 7ZT
Shareholders: Martin William Smith; Gillian Margaret Burgis-Smith
Officers: Gillian Burgis [1968] Director/Architect; Martin William Smith [1966] Director/Brewer

Brute Brewing Company Ltd
Incorporated: 5 April 2017
Registered Office: 9 Slievecorragh Avenue, Newcastle, Co Down, BT33 0JA
Major Shareholder: David Andrew Irvine
Officers: David Andrew Irvine [1983] Director/Chef

Bullington End Cider Limited
Incorporated: 20 August 2010
Net Worth Deficit: £2,113 *Total Assets:* £1,153
Registered Office: New Buildings Farm, Bullington End, Hanslope, Bucks, MK19 7BQ
Major Shareholder: David Paul Webber
Officers: David Paul Webber [1965] Director

H P Bulmer Limited
Incorporated: 27 June 1918
Net Worth: £120,968,000 *Total Assets:* £182,007,000
Registered Office: Elsley Court, 20-22 Great Titchfield Street, London, W1W 8BE
Parent: Scottish & Newcastle Limited
Officers: David Michael Forde [1968] Managing Director [Irish]; Lynsey Jane Nicoll [1980] Director/Lawyer; Radovan Sikorsky [1967] Finance Director [Slovak]; Kelly Taylor-Welsh [1978] Director/Head of UK Tax

Bumble Mead Ltd
Incorporated: 1 February 2019
Registered Office: 18 The Causeway, Chippenham, Wilts, SN15 3DB
Major Shareholder: Thomas Edward Jenner
Officers: Thomas Edward Jenner [1985] Director/Dreyman

Bygumpty Limited
Incorporated: 7 November 2005
Net Worth Deficit: £3,163 *Total Assets:* £4,238
Registered Office: 9 Nellive Park, St Brides, Wentlooge, Newport, NP10 8SE
Shareholder: William Picton
Officers: Dr William Picton, Secretary/Micro Brewer; Ann Picton [1949] Director/Headteacher; Dr William Picton [1948] Director/Micro Brewer; Ceri Picton Tully [1974] Director/IT Project Manager; Steven Richard Tully [1969] Director/Plumber

Cairn O'Mohr Ltd.
Incorporated: 25 October 2002 *Employees:* 10
Net Worth: £122,576 *Total Assets:* £481,999
Registered Office: East Inchmichael Farm, Errol, Perth, PH2 7SP
Shareholders: Judith May Gillies; Ronald Andrew Gillies
Officers: Judith Gillies, Secretary; Judith Gillies [1961] Director/Fruit Wine Maker; Ronald Andrew Gillies [1957] Director/Manager

Caledonia Cider Limited
Incorporated: 23 February 2017
Net Worth Deficit: £14,448 *Total Assets:* £23,879
Registered Office: East Adamston Farm, Muirhead, Dundee, DD2 5QX
Shareholders: Fiona Patricia Morrison; Andrew James Husband
Officers: Iain Sydney Russell Baird, Secretary; Andrew James Husband [1967] Director; Angus Kennedy Morrison [1961] Director

Caledonian Cider Company Limited
Incorporated: 10 April 2017
Registered Office: Clover Cottage, Burnside Lane, Conon Bridge, Dingwall, Highland, IV7 8EX
Major Shareholder: Ryan Ray Sealey
Officers: Ryan Ray Sealey [1981] Director/Cider Maker

Calmcorn Ltd
Incorporated: 18 July 2018
Registered Office: Suite 6, First Floor, Wordsworth Mill, Wordsworth Street, Bolton, Lancs, BL1 3ND
Major Shareholder: Anna Estocakova
Officers: Alan Edioma [1970] Director [Filipino]

Caneys Cider Ltd
Incorporated: 17 October 2018
Registered Office: 3 Foster Avenue, Studley, Warwicks, B80 7QJ
Officers: John Edward Caney [1970] Director/Cider Producer; Victoria Anne Caney [1980] Director/Cider Producer

Caxdon Premier Limited
Incorporated: 21 July 2017
Registered Office: 14-16 Powis Street, London, SE18 6LF
Major Shareholder: Donald Toseafa
Officers: Caroline Toseafa [1969] Director/Healthcare Practitioner; Donald Toseafa [1962] Director/Psychiatric Practitioner

Celtic Marches Beverages Ltd
Incorporated: 16 August 2010 *Employees:* 4
Net Worth Deficit: £211,600 *Total Assets:* £203,197
Registered Office: St Eloys, 22 Farley Road, Malvern, Worcs, WR14 1NF
Shareholders: Susan Jeanette Vaughan; Robert James Hancocks
Officers: Darren John Morris, Secretary; Robert James Hancocks [1967] Director/Farmer; Darren John Morris [1968] Director/Banking; Christopher James Palmes [1968] Operations Director; Susan Jeanette Vaughan [1962] Director/Self Employed

Chalice Mead Limited
Incorporated: 2 September 2015
Net Worth: £693 *Total Assets:* £24,815
Registered Office: 6th Floor, Amp House, Dingwall Road, Croydon, Surrey, CR0 2LX
Major Shareholder: Michael David Wagstaff
Officers: Michael David Wagstaff [1964] Director/Sales Executive

Chase Cider Limited
Incorporated: 18 December 2013
Registered Office: 31 Barton Gate, Barton under Needwood, Burton on Trent, Staffs, DE13 8AG
Major Shareholder: Neale Antony Buckland
Officers: Neale Antony Buckland [1958] Director/Owner

The Cheltenham Cider Company Ltd
Incorporated: 28 February 2019
Registered Office: 4 Sandhurst Place, London Road, Charlton Kings, Cheltenham, Glos, GL52 6YN
Major Shareholder: James Matthew Earle
Officers: James Matthew Earle [1970] Director

The Chiltern Cider Company Limited
Incorporated: 21 September 2015
Registered Office: Furzefield Farm, Furzefield Lane, Lee Gate, Great Missenden, Bucks, HP16 9NR
Shareholders: Dominic Knight Cheetham; Bryan Seymour Hart
Officers: Dominic Knight Cheetham [1967] Director; Bryan Seymour Hart [1957] Director

Chucklehead Cider Ltd
Incorporated: 15 January 2010
Net Worth: £61,369 *Total Assets:* £71,706
Registered Office: Lucerne, Broad Road, Nutbourne, Chichester, W Sussex, PO18 8SW
Shareholders: Elizabeth Claire Dinnage; Michael John Dinnage
Officers: Elizabeth Claire Dinnage [1962] Director/Cidermaker; Michael John Dinnage [1960] Director/Cidermaker

Cider Brandy Ltd
Incorporated: 8 July 2004
Net Worth Deficit: £4,561
Registered Office: c/o Francis Clark LLP, North Quay House, Sutton Harbour, Plymouth, PL4 0RA
Major Shareholder: Stephen John Mittler
Officers: Stephen John Mittler, Secretary; Stephen John Mittler [1959] Director

Cider Mill Limited
Incorporated: 7 October 2018
Registered Office: Studio Graphene, Huckletree, 18 Finsbury Square, London, EC2A 1AH
Major Shareholder: Ritam Gandhi
Officers: Ritam Gandhi [1984] Director

Cidre Bouche UK Limited
Incorporated: 2 November 2011
Net Worth: £22,500 *Total Assets:* £22,500
Registered Office: Slepe Farm, Slepe, Poole, Dorset, BH16 6HS
Major Shareholder: Andrew Charles Selby Bennett
Officers: James Sebastian Selby Bennett, Secretary; Andrew Charles Selby Bennett [1982] Director

The Clandestine Distillery Limited
Incorporated: 21 December 2018
Registered Office: Low Barn, Llancayo Business Park, Usk, Monmouthshire, NP15 1HY
Shareholders: Nathan Edward Thompson; Sarah Thompson
Officers: Nathan Edward Thompson [1978] Director

Colemans Cider Company Limited
Incorporated: 5 March 2015
Net Worth: £12,095 *Total Assets:* £38,398
Registered Office: Eastgate House, East Street, Kilham, Driffield, E Yorks, YO25 4RE
Shareholder: Marc Andrew Richard Cole
Officers: Jodie Alison Haines, Secretary; Marc Andrew Richard Cole [1963] Director; Steven Jackson [1965] Director/Cider Maker; Harmesh Lal Jassal [1966] Director

Colourful Outbursts Limited
Incorporated: 27 April 2017
Net Worth Deficit: £6,162 *Total Assets:* £14,395
Registered Office: 6 Red Cross Road, Goring on Thames, Oxon, RG8 9HG
Officers: James Dawe, Secretary; James Dawe [1976] Director/Cider Maker; Timothy Schulz [1980] Director/Cider Maker

Conte International Limited
Incorporated: 30 March 2015
Registered Office: Morbec Lodge, Arterial Road, Wickford, Essex, SS12 9JF
Major Shareholder: Marko Conte
Officers: Marko Conte [1984] Director/Motor Trade

Cooks Cider Ltd
Incorporated: 28 November 2017
Registered Office: Ivy House, Farm Tilton Road, Twyford, Melton Mowbray, Leics, LE14 2HZ
Major Shareholder: Hiranthi Geraldine Cook
Officers: Hiranthi Cook, Secretary; Hiranthi Generaldine Cook [1971] Director/Cider Producer; Matthew Cook [1968] Director/Cider Producer; Sebastian Cook [2001] Director/Cider Producer

Cool Brew Dept Ltd
Incorporated: 26 June 2018
Registered Office: Flat 2, 134 Valley Drive, Harrogate, N Yorks, HG2 0JS
Major Shareholder: Matthew Leonard Edgar
Officers: Matthew Leonard Edgar [1984] Director

The Copse House Cider Company Ltd
Incorporated: 22 November 2013
Net Worth Deficit: £197,983 *Total Assets:* £25,231
Registered Office: New Barn Yard, Sandley, Gillingham, Dorset, SP8 5DZ
Major Shareholder: Oliver Reginald Tant
Officers: Oliver Reginald Tant [1961] Director/Chartered Accountant

The Core Cider Company Limited
Incorporated: 7 July 2017
Registered Office: Brundish House, The Street, Woodbridge, Suffolk, IP13 8BL
Shareholders: Marc Adrian Longe; Danke Longe
Officers: Danke Longe [1968] Director; Marc Adrian Longe [1956] Director

Cornish Mead Co.Limited
Incorporated: 16 May 1957 *Employees:* 5
Net Worth: £1,048,710 *Total Assets:* £1,858,961
Registered Office: The Mead House, Mount Prospect Terrace, Newlyn, Penzance, Cornwall, TR18 5QF
Major Shareholder: Sidney Thomas Leiworthy
Officers: Matthew Leiworthy, Secretary; Sophia Emma Fenton [1966] Director/Restaurateur; Matthew Thomas Leiworthy [1967] Director/Restaurateur; Sidney Thomas Leiworthy [1938] Director

Cornish Orchards Ltd
Incorporated: 19 August 2003 *Employees:* 36
Net Worth: £867,706 *Total Assets:* £2,721,597
Registered Office: Griffin Brewery, Chiswick Lane South, Chiswick, London, W4 2QB
Parent: Fuller, Smith & Turner P.L.C.
Officers: Severine Pascale Bequin, Secretary; Simon Ray Dodd [1974] Director; Simon Emeny [1965] Director/Chairman; Richard Hamilton Fleetwood Fuller [1960] Director; Jonathon David Swaine [1971] Director

Cornish Scrumpy Company Limited
Incorporated: 6 November 1979 *Employees:* 61
Net Worth: £439,914 *Total Assets:* £3,795,550
Registered Office: 7 Sandy Court, Ashleigh Way, Langage Business Park, Plymouth, PL7 5JX
Parent: Cornish Scrumpy Holdings Limited
Officers: Kay Victoria Healey, Secretary; David John Healey [1956] Director; Jonathon Healey [1986] Director; Kay Victoria Healey [1957] Director/Company Secretary; Sam Healey [1985] Director

Cornish Scrumpy Holdings Limited
Incorporated: 24 April 2001 *Employees:* 2
Net Worth: £8,857,481 *Total Assets:* £10,185,911
Registered Office: 7 Sandy Court, Ashleigh Way, Langage Business Park, Plymouth, PL7 5JX
Parent: Healey Holdings Limited
Officers: Kay Victoria Healey, Secretary; David John Healey [1956] Director; Jonathon Healey [1986] Director; Kay Victoria Healey [1957] Director; Sam Healey [1985] Director

Cornwall Cider Co. Limited
Incorporated: 22 October 2013 *Employees:* 3
Net Worth Deficit: £1,744 *Total Assets:* £62,024
Registered Office: c/o Bishop Fleming, Chy Nyverow, Newham Road, Truro, Cornwall, TR1 2DP
Shareholders: Alun David Morgan; Michael Brian Pritchard; Steven John Skinner
Officers: Alun David Morgan [1967] Director; Michael Brian Pritchard [1968] Director; Steven John Skinner [1956] Director

The Cotswold Cider Company Ltd
Incorporated: 12 December 2009
Net Worth: £153,283 *Total Assets:* £259,583
Registered Office: 54 Coleshill, Swindon, Wilts, SN6 7PT
Major Shareholder: Rory Julian Souter
Officers: Juliet Souter, Secretary; James David Cameron Douglas-Hamilton [1964] Director/Financial Adviser; Fergus Giles Anthony Mitchell [1964] Director; Rory Julian Souter [1967] Managing Director

The Cotswold Fruit Company Ltd.
Incorporated: 20 November 2014
Net Worth Deficit: £49,867 *Total Assets:* £17,607
Registered Office: Bleby House, Abbey Terrace, Winchcombe, Cheltenham, Glos, GL54 5LL
Major Shareholder: David Richard Lindgren
Officers: Frances Bryony House [1966] Director; David Richard Lindgren [1961] Business Development Director

Covenflare Ltd
Incorporated: 8 June 2018
Registered Office: Suite 1, Fielden House, 41 Rochdale Road, Todmorden, W Yorks, OL14 6LD
Shareholders: Albert Sawit; Jodie McClelland
Officers: Albert Sawit [1980] Director [Filipino]

Craft Cider Limited
Incorporated: 6 February 2019
Registered Office: Beaumont House, 172 Southgate Street, Gloucester, GL1 2EZ
Major Shareholder: James Alistair McCrindle
Officers: James Alistair McCrindle [1973] Director

Craftwater Brewing Company Limited
Incorporated: 23 July 2018
Registered Office: 11 Moorsend, Kingsteignton, Newton Abbot, Devon, TQ12 3JY
Shareholders: Russell Stanley Nixon; Christopher James Thackray; Christopher Andrew Ward
Officers: Christopher James Thackray [1983] Managing Director

Crai Cider Company Limited
Incorporated: 19 September 2018
Registered Office: Pentwyn Uchaf, Crai, Brecon, Powys, LD3 8YN
Shareholders: Stephen Kinghan; Anneka Kinghan
Officers: Anneka Kinghan [1985] Director; Stephen Kinghan [1983] Director

Cranes Drink Ltd
Incorporated: 5 August 2013
Net Worth Deficit: £36,217 *Total Assets:* £153,917
Registered Office: Top Farm, Lower Road, Croydon, Royston, Herts, SG8 0EQ
Shareholders: Daniel James Ritsema; Benjamin Lee Ritsema
Officers: Ivor John Anthony Harrison [1965] Director; Benjamin Lee Ritsema [1990] Director/Manufacturer of Alcoholic Cranberry Drink; Daniel James Ritsema [1990] Director/Manufacturer of Alcoholic Cranberry Drink

Crazy Dave's Cider Ltd
Incorporated: 26 May 2016
Registered Office: 6 Altmore, Cherry Garden Lane, Maidenhead, Berks, SL6 3QG
Major Shareholder: David Philip Snowden
Officers: David Philip Snowden [1970] Director/Cider Maker

Creoda's Hill Ltd
Incorporated: 9 February 2016 *Employees:* 1
Net Worth Deficit: £2,447 *Total Assets:* £5,509
Registered Office: Horse Shoe House, Horse Shoe Lane, Wootton, Woodstock, Oxon, OX20 1DR
Major Shareholder: Matthew Bennett Rippon
Officers: Matthew Bennett Rippon [1968] Director

Crosby Beverages Ltd
Incorporated: 19 February 2018
Registered Office: 193 Drayton Bridge Road, London, W13 0JH
Major Shareholder: Odi Olali
Officers: Rhys Johnson [1991] Director; Odi Olali [1990] Director

The Crossroads Brewery Limited
Incorporated: 7 April 2018
Registered Office: 70 Park Avenue, Washington, Tyne & Wear, NE37 2QS
Major Shareholder: Christopher Thomas Mitchinson
Officers: Christopher Thomas Mitchinson [1987] Director

Dampney's Remarkable Drinks Ltd.
Incorporated: 29 April 2015
Registered Office: Gowans, East Meon, Petersfield, Hants, GU32 1HT
Major Shareholder: Jonathan Nicholas Dampney
Officers: Jonathan Nicholas Dampney [1989] Director; Richard John Dampney [1957] Director

Damsons in Distress Limited
Incorporated: 20 February 2009
Registered Office: Binbrook Hill Farm, Binbrook Hill, Binbrook, Market Rasen, Lincs, LN8 6BL
Major Shareholder: Phillipa Nickerson Gloeckner
Officers: Phillipa Nickerson Gloeckner [1980] Director/Solicitor

Darley Abbey Cider Company Limited
Incorporated: 15 March 2016
Net Worth Deficit: £4,885 *Total Assets:* £11,678
Registered Office: 12 Darley Abbey Mills, Darley Abbey, Derby, DE22 1DZ
Shareholders: Philippa Worsey; Simon Worsey
Officers: Simon Worsey [1968] Director

Dean Press Cider Ltd.
Incorporated: 17 October 2017
Registered Office: Underdean House, Newnham Road, Blakeney, Norfolk, GL15 4AE
Major Shareholder: Christopher Michael Peter Fordham
Officers: Christopher Michael Peter Fordham [1983] Director

Dee Ciders Limited
Incorporated: 7 February 2014
Net Worth Deficit: £1,690 *Total Assets:* £7,398
Registered Office: Unit 1b The Old Chapel, Denbigh Road, Hendre, Mold, Flintshire, CH7 5QL
Shareholders: Christopher Scott Johnson; Richard Michael Johnson
Officers: Christopher Scott Johnson [1978] Director; Richard Michael Johnson [1952] Director

Diamations Ltd
Incorporated: 24 May 2018
Registered Office: 129 Burnley Road, Padiham, Burnley, Lancs, BB12 8BA
Shareholders: Jhonafe David; Paul Noble
Officers: Jhonafe David [1985] Director [Filipino]

Distell International Holdings Limited
Incorporated: 8 April 2016
Net Worth: £16,970,308 *Total Assets:* £18,152,844
Registered Office: Avalon House, 72 Lower Mortlake Road, Richmond, Surrey, TW9 2JY
Parent: Distell Group Limited
Officers: Nwavudu Constance Ekebuisi, Secretary; Christopher John Blandford-Newson [1964] Director/Asset Management [British/South African]; Steven Jeffrey Nathan [1962] Director [South African]; Werner Nolte [1976] Finance Director [South African]; Fraser John Thornton [1969] Managing Director; Leonard Jacobus Volschenk [1971] Managing Director [South African]

DJ Wines Limited
Incorporated: 18 May 2016 *Employees:* 2
Net Worth: £5,437 *Total Assets:* £57,362
Registered Office: Unit 3 The Winery, School Road, Monk Soham, Woodbridge, Suffolk, IP13 7EN
Shareholders: Derek Ian Jones; Richard Neil Jones
Officers: Richard Neil Jones, Secretary; Derek Ian Jones [1957] Director/Wine Maker; Richard Neil Jones [1957] Director/Accountant/IT

The Donhead Apple Company Ltd
Incorporated: 14 November 2011
Net Worth Deficit: £28,454 *Total Assets:* £43,592
Registered Office: The Croft, Berrywood Lane, Donhead St Mary, Shaftesbury, Dorset, SP7 9DH
Major Shareholder: Gavin Tait
Officers: Gavin Tait [1970] Director/Financial Consultant

Dorset Orchards Limited
Incorporated: 4 July 2014
Registered Office: c/o JC & RH Palmer Ltd, Old Brewery, Bridport, Dorset, DT6 4JA
Parent: JC & RH Palmer Limited
Officers: Gary George Adcock [1963] Director/Accountant; Anthony John Cleeves Palmer [1951] Director; Cleeves William Robert Palmer [1962] Director

The Dower House Cider Company Ltd.
Incorporated: 9 January 2012
Registered Office: The Dower House, Church Lane, Forthampton, Gloucester, GL19 4QW
Major Shareholder: Keith Richard Norton
Officers: Keith Richard Norton [1955] Director/Management Consultant

Drapex Ltd
Incorporated: 1 June 2018
Registered Office: Office 3, 146-148 Bury Old Road, Whitefield, Manchester, M45 6AT
Shareholders: Kathleen Ann Vizcarra; Carly Rigby
Officers: Kathleen Ann Vizcarra [1995] Director [Filipino]

Duckchicken Limited
Incorporated: 8 April 2017
Net Worth: £437 *Total Assets:* £5,437
Registered Office: 57 Credenhill Street, London, SW16 6PP
Shareholders: James Mann; Colleen O'Sullivan
Officers: James Mann, Secretary; James Mann [1987] Director/Cider Maker; Colleen O'Sullivan [1982] Director/Cider Maker [American]

Dudda's Tun Ltd
Incorporated: 11 September 2013 *Employees:* 2
Net Worth: £58,564 *Total Assets:* £114,328
Registered Office: Pine Trees Farm, Bistock, Doddington, Sittingbourne, Kent, ME9 0AX
Shareholders: Kevin Payne; Robert John Payne
Officers: Kevin Payne [1955] Director/Farmer; Robert John Payne [1983] Director/Farmer

Dunkertons Cider Company Limited
Incorporated: 15 September 2000 *Employees:* 11
Net Worth Deficit: £55,027 *Total Assets:* £881,020
Registered Office: Dowdeswell Park, London Road, Charlton Kings, Cheltenham, Glos, GL52 6UT
Shareholders: Julian Marc Dunkerton; Jeremy Benson
Officers: Jeremy Benson [1971] Director; Julian Marc Dunkerton [1965] Director

Dunwrights Cider Company Ltd
Incorporated: 5 October 2018
Registered Office: 20a Racecommon Road, Barnsley, S Yorks, S70 1BH
Major Shareholder: Aleksandra Maria Habich-Crayton
Officers: Aleksandra Maria Habich-Crayton [1979] Director [Polish]

Duxford Scrumpy Company Limited
Incorporated: 25 April 2016 *Employees:* 3
Net Worth: £710 *Total Assets:* £3,733
Registered Office: 115c Milton Road, Cambridge, CB4 1XE
Shareholders: Kay Dawn Jagels; Stephen William Martin; Oliver Nentwich
Officers: Kay Dawn Jagels [1971] Director/Materials Manager; Stephen William Martin [1975] Director/Scientist [American]; Oliver Nentwich [1971] Director/Scientist [German]

East Coast Cider Company Limited
Incorporated: 15 May 2018
Registered Office: 402 Chillingham Road, Newcastle upon Tyne, NE6 5QX
Major Shareholder: Tim Woolley
Officers: Katherine Ruth Comer [1987] Director; Tim Woolley [1982] Director/Cider Maker

East Norfolk Trading Company Limited
Incorporated: 16 April 2009
Net Worth: £25,654 *Total Assets:* £89,140
Registered Office: 15 Station Road, Ormesby, Great Yarmouth, Norfolk, NR29 3NH
Major Shareholder: Russell James Watson
Officers: Sally Watson, Secretary; Russell James Watson [1964] Director/Builder; Sally Watson [1967] Director

Eastern Cider House Ltd.
Incorporated: 6 February 2018
Registered Office: 33 Mayflower Road, London, SW9 9JY
Shareholders: Anna Skyner; Louis Skyner
Officers: Anna Skyner [1980] Director/Founder [Russian]

Embev Ltd
Incorporated: 16 May 2018
Registered Office: Flat 3, 162 Cambridge Street, London, SW1V 4QE
Major Shareholder: Matthew Nicolas Clark
Officers: Matthew Nicolas Clark [1990] Director/Entrepreneur

Essex Cider Company Limited
Incorporated: 16 June 2014
Net Worth: £1,000 *Total Assets:* £1,000
Registered Office: The Falcon, High Street, Wivenhoe, Colchester, Essex, CO7 9BE
Shareholders: Gregor James Grant; James Richard Stevens
Officers: Gregor James Grant [1974] Director/Forensic Scientist; James Richard Stevens [1970] Director

Evopan Ltd
Incorporated: 25 June 2018
Registered Office: Suite 1, Fielden House, 41 Rochdale Road, Todmorden, W Yorks, OL14 6LD
Shareholders: Donna Mae Sumog Oy; Charlotte Henshaw
Officers: Donna Mae Sumog Oy [1992] Director [Filipino]

Farcial Ltd
Incorporated: 28 April 2018
Registered Office: 129 Burnley Road, Padiham, Burnley, Lancs, BB12 8BA
Shareholders: Clarita Bellena; Claire Ambrose
Officers: Clarita Bellena [1964] Director [Filipino]

The Fermentorium Ltd
Incorporated: 9 October 2015 *Employees:* 1
Net Worth Deficit: £3,856 *Total Assets:* £3,308
Registered Office: First Floor, Thavies Inn House, 3-4 Holborn Circus, London, EC1N 2HA
Major Shareholder: Kevin Hurdwell
Officers: Kevin Hurdwell [1959] Director

Festival Beverage and Property Services Limited
Incorporated: 18 April 2018
Registered Office: 63 Oxgangs Road, Edinburgh, EH10 7BD
Major Shareholder: Craig John Murray
Officers: Craig John Murray [1958] Director/Writer

The Flower Miners Limited
Incorporated: 8 January 2019
Registered Office: Trevella, Trispen, Truro, Cornwall, TR4 9BD
Major Shareholder: Anne-Marie Hurst
Officers: Anne-Marie Hurst [1965] Director

Frampton Farm Limited
Incorporated: 11 July 2007
Net Worth Deficit: £33,639 *Total Assets:* £187
Registered Office: 117-119 Temple Chambers, Temple Avenue, London, EC4Y 0HP
Major Shareholder: Timothy Robert Johnson
Officers: Timothy Robert Johnson [1949] Director/Solicitor

Fruito Soft Drinks Limited
Incorporated: 25 June 2018
Registered Office: 65 Samuel Street, London, SE18 5LF
Parent: Topmost Foods Limited
Officers: Adekunle Akanji Ademola [1955] Director

The Garden Cider Company Limited
Incorporated: 1 December 2010
Net Worth Deficit: £49,484 *Total Assets:* £440,612
Registered Office: Unit 4 Ardington Courtyard, Roke Lane, Witley, Godalming, Surrey, GU8 5NF
Shareholder: Benjamin Filby
Officers: Neville Patrick Bryan [1963] Director/Businessman; Benjamin James Filby [1972] Director; William Jack Filby [1974] Director; Maureen Heffernan [1960] Director; Dave Rogers [1951] Director/Businessman; Jonathan David Philip Stevens [1959] Director/Solicitor

Gaymer Cider Company Limited
Incorporated: 8 July 2009
Registered Office: Ashford House, Grenadier Road, Exeter, Devon, EX1 3LH
Parent: C & C Group PLC
Officers: Stephen Glancey [1960] Director; Riona Heffernan [1980] Director/Chartered Accountant [Irish]; Ewan James Robertson [1982] Director/Accountant

The Gentleman's Cider Ltd.
Incorporated: 24 October 2018
Registered Office: 34b Marryat Square, Wyfold Road, London, SW6 6UA
Major Shareholder: George Peter Dyer
Officers: George Peter Dyer [1992] Director/Chef

Giggler Ltd
Incorporated: 28 April 2015
Net Worth: £608 *Total Assets:* £14,038
Registered Office: 2 Dunston Street, London, E8 4EB
Major Shareholder: Timothy James Chapman
Officers: Timothy James Chapman, Secretary; Timothy James Chapman [1962] Director

Ginomine Ltd
Incorporated: 22 July 2018
Registered Office: 214a Kettering Road, Northampton, NN1 4BN
Shareholders: Mary Grace Orbello; Jodie McClelland
Officers: Mary Grace Orbello [1989] Director [Filipino]

Ginsecco Ltd
Incorporated: 12 October 2018
Registered Office: 17 Whitelaw Street, Glasgow, G20 0DG
Shareholders: Jonathan McCall; Craig Gibson
Officers: Craig Gibson [1983] Director/Engineer; Jonathan McCall [1982] Director/Engineer

The Glastonbury Drinks Company Limited
Incorporated: 17 February 2017
Registered Office: Cooper House, Lower Charlton Trading Estate, Shepton Mallet, Somerset, BA4 5QE
Shareholders: Christopher Edgar Hecks; Sandra Pamela Hecks
Officers: Christopher Edgar Hecks [1965] Director; Sandra Pamela Hecks [1967] Director

Goodness Sake Limited
Incorporated: 9 January 2014
Registered Office: Basement Flat, 7 Park Crescent, Brighton, BN2 3HA
Officers: Simon John Lees Reed [1973] Director/Systems Analyst; Helen Elizabeth Ross [1962] Director/Carer

Gospel Green Cyder Company Limited
Incorporated: 30 August 2016
Net Worth: £1 *Total Assets:* £1
Registered Office: Low Barn, Llancayo Business Park, Usk, Monmouthshire, NP15 1HY
Major Shareholder: Brock Ninian Sanderson Bergius
Officers: Brock Ninian Sanderson Bergius [1977] Director

Green and Pleasant London Limited
Incorporated: 1 September 2014
Net Worth Deficit: £200,780 *Total Assets:* £14,379
Registered Office: Quern House, Mill Court, Great Shelford, Cambridge, CB22 5LD
Major Shareholder: Andrew Murray
Officers: Andrew Murray [1962] Director

The Green Shed Cider Company Limited
Incorporated: 15 January 2018
Registered Office: 100 Craven Road, Newbury, Berks, RG14 5NP
Major Shareholder: David Bailey
Officers: David Bailey [1967] Director/Civil Engineer

Green Valley Cyder Limited
Incorporated: 27 July 2018
Registered Office: Haines Watts, Parliament Square, Parliament Street, Crediton, Devon, EX17 2AW
Officers: William Butterfield [1977] Director/Cider Maker

Grumpy Frog Ltd
Incorporated: 31 October 2016
Registered Office: Puddocks, Frog Lane, Ilmington, Shipston on Stour, Warwicks, CV36 4LQ
Major Shareholder: William Howard Buckley
Officers: William Howard Buckley [1941] Director/Chartered Accountant

Grumpy Wasp Ltd
Incorporated: 22 March 2018
Registered Office: Rosedean Farm, Mark Lane, East Markhan, Newark, Notts, NG22 0QU
Major Shareholder: Timothy Paul Needham
Officers: Timothy Paul Needham [1960] Director/Brewer

Gwatkin Cider Co. Limited
Incorporated: 30 July 2003
Net Worth Deficit: £37,150 *Total Assets:* £156,326
Registered Office: Golden Valley Accountancy, Westwood Industrial Estate, Pontrilas, Herefords, HR2 0EL
Major Shareholder: Denis Edward Charles Gwatkin
Officers: Denis Edward Charles Gwatkin [1969] Director; Eric William John Gwatkin [1965] Director; Theresa Roberts [1967] Director

Gwynt y Ddraig Cider Ltd
Incorporated: 22 June 2004 *Employees:* 15
Net Worth: £739,847 *Total Assets:* £1,099,830
Registered Office: Llest Farmhouse, Llantwit Fardre, Pontypridd, Rhondda Cynon Taf, CF38 2PW
Parent: The Cider & Perry Company (Wales) Ltd
Officers: Lyn Howell Casling [1953] Director/Accountant; Ian Evans [1953] Director/Distiller; Andrew Gronow [1966] Director/Welder

H & A Prestige Bottling Limited
Incorporated: 19 October 1983 *Employees:* 178
Net Worth: £2,822,000 *Total Assets:* £11,142,000
Registered Office: The Winery, Ackhurst Road, Ackhurst Business Park, Chorley, Lancs, PR7 1NH
Shareholders: Judith Margaret Halewood; Ian Alan Douglas; Halewood Wines and Spirits PLC
Officers: Ian Alan Douglas [1951] Director; Peter Gary Eaton [1960] Director; Stewart Andrew Hainsworth [1969] Director/Chief Executive; Judith Margaret Halewood [1951] Director; Daniel Mark Kirwin [1959] Director; Alan William Robinson [1965] Director/Accountant; Lee Andrew Tayburn [1974] Director of Production

Halewood International Limited
Incorporated: 7 February 2000 *Employees:* 315
Net Worth: £13,086,000 *Total Assets:* £97,916,000
Registered Office: The Sovereign Distillery, Wilson Road, Huyton Business Park, Knowsley, Merseyside, L36 6AD
Parent: Halewood International Holdings (UK) Limited
Officers: John Andrew Bradbury [1971] Managing Director; Peter Gary Eaton [1960] Director; Timothy Robert Goff [1973] Purchasing Director; Stewart Andrew Hainsworth [1969] Director/Chief Executive Officer; Judith Margaret Halewood [1951] Director; Timothy Richard Hines [1979] Finance Director; Alan William Robinson [1965] Director/Accountant; Lee Andrew Tayburn [1974] Director of Production

The Halfpenny Green Cider Company Limited
Incorporated: 7 December 2016
Registered Office: 23 Dark Lane, Kinver, Staffs, DY7 6JB
Shareholders: Anthony James Lovering; Malcolm Ernest Braham
Officers: Malcolm Ernest Braham [1959] Director; Anthony James Lovering [1958] Director

Halorank Ltd
Incorporated: 25 May 2018
Registered Office: 129 Burnley Road, Padiham, Burnley, Lancs, BB12 8BA
Shareholders: Emilia Roldan; Rochelle Cleminshaw
Officers: Emilia Roldan [1962] Director [Filipino]

Ham Hill Cider Limited
Incorporated: 1 June 2012
Net Worth: £2,757 *Total Assets:* £21,862
Registered Office: Ham Hill Cider, North Down Farm, Haselbury Plucknett, Crewkerne, Somerset, TA18 7PL
Officers: Neil Chapillon [1970] Director/Building Surveyor; Mark Edmonds [1968] Director/Skilled Roadworker; Christopher Worledge [1971] Director/Lecturer; Simon Worledge [1968] Director/Project Manager

Hampshire Downs Fine Cider Company Ltd
Incorporated: 20 June 2013
Net Worth Deficit: £109,771 *Total Assets:* £101,589
Registered Office: 9 Christchurch Road, Winchester, Hants, SO23 9SR
Major Shareholder: Piotr Jan Nahajski
Officers: Piotr Jan Nahajski [1961] Director

Handmade Cider Company Limited
Incorporated: 4 May 2010 *Employees:* 1
Net Worth Deficit: £4,601 *Total Assets:* £40,447
Registered Office: The Old Cider Shed, Slaughterford Mill, Slaughterford, Chippenham, Wilts, SN14 8RJ
Major Shareholder: Denis France
Officers: Denis France [1967] Director

Thomas Hardy Burtonwood Limited
Incorporated: 10 July 1998 *Employees:* 43
Net Worth: £468,000 *Total Assets:* £6,525,000
Registered Office: Bold Lane, Burtonwood, Warrington, Cheshire, WA5 4TH
Officers: Gary Alexander Todd [1966] Site Director; Neil Mark Voss [1969] Director; Jonathan Christopher Ward [1978] Director; Margaret Rae Ward [1944] Director

Thomas Hardy Holdings Limited
Incorporated: 27 December 1996 *Employees:* 114
Net Worth: £12,852,000 *Total Assets:* £19,423,000
Registered Office: Bold Lane, Burtonwood, Warrington, Cheshire, WA5 4TH
Officers: Neil Mark Voss [1969] Director; Jonathan Christopher Ward [1978] Director; Margaret Rae Ward [1944] Director

Thomas Hardy Kendal Limited
Incorporated: 29 December 1998 *Employees:* 64
Net Worth: £6,922,000 *Total Assets:* £9,162,000
Registered Office: Bold Lane, Burtonwood, Warrington, Cheshire, WA5 4TH
Officers: Peter Michael Armstrong [1965] Site Director; Neil Mark Voss [1969] Director; Jonathan Christopher Ward [1978] Director; Margaret Rae Ward [1944] Director

Harleston Cider Company Limited
Incorporated: 27 September 2016 *Employees:* 2
Net Worth Deficit: £47,673 *Total Assets:* £23,330
Registered Office: 6 Recreation Walk, Harleston, Norfolk, IP20 9BX
Shareholders: Tim Woolley; Ruth Comer
Officers: Ruth Comer, Secretary; Ruth Comer [1987] Director; Deb Woolley [1954] Director; Ken Woolley [1951] Director; Tim Woolley [1982] Director

Harnser Enterprises Ltd
Incorporated: 17 October 2014
Net Worth: £43,718 *Total Assets:* £53,813
Registered Office: 9 John Childs Way, Bungay, Suffolk, NR35 1SE
Shareholder: Christopher Hurle Morshead
Officers: Christopher Hurle Morshead [1961] Director/Aero Engineer

The Harrogate Cider Company Limited
Incorporated: 21 July 2016 *Employees:* 2
Net Worth Deficit: £3,866 *Total Assets:* £88,584
Registered Office: 5 Lockwood Close, Leeds, LS11 5UU
Shareholders: Paul Waterton; Corrine Elaine Waterton
Officers: Corrine Elaine Waterton [1963] Director; Paul Waterton [1964] Director

Harry's Cider Company Limited
Incorporated: 12 March 2012 *Employees:* 3
Net Worth: £35,070 *Total Assets:* £159,295
Registered Office: 10 South Street, Bridport, Dorset, DT6 3NJ
Major Shareholder: Harry Stewart Fry
Officers: Alison Boyd Chapman [1962] Director; Harry Stewart Fry [1954] Director

Hartpury Heritage Trust
Incorporated: 6 March 1998
Net Worth: £1,184,356 *Total Assets:* £1,200,023
Registered Office: Orchard Centre, Blackwells End, Hartpury, Gloucester, GL19 3DB
Officers: Holly Bridget Chapman, Secretary; Margaret Bailey [1961] Director; Holly Bridget Chapman [1956] Museum Director; James Roger Chapman [1950] Director/Retired Solicitor; Pauline Drury [1950] Director/Teacher; John Griffiths Evans [1937] Director; Mary Rose McGhee [1935] Director/Ward Clerk

Hartpury Process Limited
Incorporated: 25 March 2015 *Employees:* 2
Net Worth: £2,876 *Total Assets:* £8,381
Registered Office: The Orchard Centre, Blackwell's End, Hartpury, Gloucester, GL19 3DB
Officers: James Roger Chapman, Secretary; Holly Bridget Chapman [1956] Director/Retired; James Roger Chapman [1950] Director/Retired

Hawkes Cider Limited
Incorporated: 20 September 2012 *Employees:* 9
Previous: Hawkes Brewing Company Limited
Net Worth: £429,401 *Total Assets:* £873,412
Registered Office: 92 & 96 Druid Street, London, SE1 2HQ
Parent: Brewdog PLC
Officers: Alan Martin Dickie [1982] Director; Neil Allan Simpson [1971] Director; James Bruce Watt [1982] Director; Simon Joseph Wright [1982] Managing Director

Hawkins Drinks Limited
Incorporated: 15 January 2018
Registered Office: 3 All Saints Croft, Burton on Trent, Staffs, DE14 3EA
Major Shareholder: Martin John Hawkins
Officers: Martin John Hawkins [1957] Director

Haygrove Evolution Limited
Incorporated: 17 September 2014 *Employees:* 5
Net Worth Deficit: £252,918 *Total Assets:* £842,315
Registered Office: Redbank, Little Marcle Road, Ledbury, Herefords, HR8 2JL
Major Shareholder: Angus James Davison
Officers: Richard John Mills, Secretary; Angus James Davison [1965] Director; Simon Richard Day [1970] Director; Priscilla Jane Hardwicke Sobey [1942] Director/Fruit Grower; Norman John Stanier [1947] Director/Fruit Farmer; Elizabeth Eve Waltham [1974] Director/Management Consultant

Heaton Cider Company Limited
Incorporated: 22 May 2017
Registered Office: 402 Chillingham Road, Newcastle upon Tyne, NE6 5QX
Major Shareholder: Tim Woolley
Officers: Tim Woolley [1982] Director/Cider Maker

Henney's Cider Company Limited
Incorporated: 29 May 2003 *Employees:* 1
Net Worth: £2,103,716 *Total Assets:* £2,352,033
Registered Office: 10 The Southend, Ledbury, Herefords, HR8 2EY
Major Shareholder: Michael Henney
Officers: Gwen Jabczynski, Secretary; Mike Henney [1961] Director

Heron Valley Cider Limited
Incorporated: 14 July 1997
Net Worth: £18,847 *Total Assets:* £148,672
Registered Office: 30 Fore Street, Totnes, Devon, TQ9 5RP
Shareholders: Alexander Barnaby Green; Natasha Green
Officers: Alexander Barnaby Green [1971] Director; Natasha Green [1972] Director

Hidden Orchard Ltd
Incorporated: 30 January 2019
Registered Office: Unit 1a Herniss Business Park, Longdowns, Cornwall, TR10 9BZ
Major Shareholder: Jeffrey Charles Richard Bradley
Officers: Jeffrey Charles Richard Bradley, Secretary; Jeffrey Charles Richard Bradley [1976] Director/Drinks Producer

Highland Cider Limited
Incorporated: 16 September 2014
Registered Office: Novar House, Evanton, Dingwall, Ross-shire, IV16 9XL
Officers: William Hector Luttrell Munro Ferguson [1989] Director/Highland Cider

Highworth Cider and Perry Limited
Incorporated: 30 July 2012
Net Worth Deficit: £5,496 *Total Assets:* £1,706
Registered Office: 50 Sevenfields, Highworth, Swindon, Wilts, SN6 7NF
Officers: Collin Fred [1967] Director/Telephone Engineer; David Silcock [1958] Director/Building Society Manager

Hiken Limited
Incorporated: 6 August 2003
Net Worth: £85,773 *Total Assets:* £91,612
Registered Office: 6 Recreation Walk, Harleston, Norfolk, IP20 9BX
Officers: Deborah Vine Woolley, Secretary; Deborah Vine Woolley [1954] Director/Administrator; Kenneth John Woolley [1951] Director/Chartered Engineer

Himachal Ltd
Incorporated: 7 January 2015
Net Worth: £52,827 *Total Assets:* £145,558
Registered Office: Chapel Farm, Main Street, Flawith, York, YO61 1SF
Major Shareholder: Catherine Susan White
Officers: Clive Fernandes, Secretary; Clive Fernandes [1965] Director [Indian]; David White [1963] Director/IT Distribution

Hoar Cross Cider Ltd
Incorporated: 9 March 2015
Net Worth Deficit: £21,483 *Total Assets:* £16,263
Registered Office: 24 The Meadows, Kingstone, Uttoxeter, Staffs, ST14 8QE
Shareholders: Paul Robert Mathie; Siobain Tara Mathie
Officers: Paul Robert Mathie [1957] Director/Retired Teacher; Siobain Tara Mathie [1964] Director/Accountant

Hogan's Cider Limited
Incorporated: 17 August 2005 *Employees:* 7
Net Worth Deficit: £88,689 *Total Assets:* £570,278
Registered Office: North Lodge Barn, Haselor, Alcester, Warwicks, B49 6LX
Shareholders: Allen Patrick Hogan; Jane Elizabeth Hogan
Officers: Jane Hogan, Secretary; Allen Patrick Hogan [1955] Director [Irish]

Holler Brewery Limited
Incorporated: 21 December 2017
Registered Office: 19-23 Elder Place, Brighton, BN1 4GF
Parent: Ironstone Brewery Ltd
Officers: Steve James Keegan [1982] Director; Davinder Singh Sahota [1975] Director

Honey & Daughter Limited
Incorporated: 23 April 2015
Net Worth Deficit: £3,632 *Total Assets:* £65,419
Registered Office: Lime Court, Pathfields Business Park, South Molton, Devon, EX36 3LH
Major Shareholder: Robert George Honey
Officers: Gerard Peter Coles [1969] Director/Cider Maker; Robert George Honey [1948] Director/Farmer/Cider Maker

Horse Kick Cider Ltd
Incorporated: 23 November 2016
Net Worth Deficit: £3,585 *Total Assets:* £7,217
Registered Office: Stud Office, Chasemore Farm, Bookham Road, Downside, Surrey, KT11 3JT
Major Shareholder: Patrick David Sells
Officers: Dr Patrick David Sells [1982] Director/Cider Maker

House Brewery Limited
Incorporated: 15 November 2016 *Employees:* 1
Net Worth Deficit: £14,414 *Total Assets:* £32,133
Registered Office: Southcombe Barn, Chapel Street, Axmouth, Seaton, Devon, EX12 4AN
Officers: Martin John Aberdeen [1965] Director; Tarik Ali Nashnush [1967] Director; Antony Paul Smith [1968] Director/Accountant; Dominic Stead [1968] Director/Property Developer

Hunt's Cider Limited
Incorporated: 13 June 2014
Net Worth Deficit: £5,390 *Total Assets:* £159,650
Registered Office: Broadleigh Farm, Aish Road, Stoke Gabriel, Totnes, Devon, TQ9 6PU
Shareholders: Annette Christine James; Richard George Hunt
Officers: Richard George Hunt [1981] Director; Annette Christine James [1983] Director

The Husthwaite Orchard Village Limited
Incorporated: 13 August 2009 *Employees:* 2
Net Worth: £22,120 *Total Assets:* £36,444
Registered Office: Mulberry Cottage, The Nookin, Husthwaite, York, YO61 4PY
Major Shareholder: Cameron Robertson Smith
Officers: George Anagnostopoulos [1979] Director/Cider Maker [Greek]; Cameron Robertson Smith [1951] Director/Retired

Iford Cider Limited
Incorporated: 13 October 2015
Net Worth Deficit: £13,245 *Total Assets:* £32,760
Registered Office: Iford Manor, Iford, Bradford on Avon, Wilts, BA15 2BA
Shareholders: William Fairfax Cartwright-Hignett; Joe Marley Abbott
Officers: Joe Marley Abbott [1990] Director/Brewer; Marianne Lucy Cartwright-Hignett [1983] Director/Self Employed; William Fairfax Cartwright-Hignett [1982] Director

Incubuzz Ltd
Incorporated: 25 June 2018
Registered Office: Suite 1, Fielden House, 41 Rochdale Road, Todmorden, W Yorks, OL14 6LD
Shareholders: Perla Mahinay; Darrell Brannagan
Officers: Perla Mahinay [1970] Director [Filipino]

Infirock Ltd
Incorporated: 30 April 2018
Registered Office: 129 Burnley Road, Padiham, Burnley, Lancs, BB12 8BA
Shareholders: Myla Villaroman; Leeanne McCreadie-Blake
Officers: Myla Villaroman [1969] Director [Filipino]

Islay Wines Ltd
Incorporated: 2 February 2018
Registered Office: 20-22 Wenlock Road, London, N1 7GU
Officers: Helen Isabelle Gilbert [1966] Director/Wine Producer and Seller

Isle of Islay Cider Company Ltd
Incorporated: 25 September 2018
Registered Office: 5 Lennox Street, Port Ellen, Islay, Argyll, PA42 7BT
Major Shareholder: Kevin Heads
Officers: Kevin Heads [1978] Director/Distillery Operator

Isle of Mull Winery Ltd
Incorporated: 20 October 2017
Registered Office: 9 Rockfield Road, Tobermory, Isle of Mull, PA75 6PN
Major Shareholder: Donald Alexander Holmes
Officers: Donald Alexander Holmes [1965] Company Secretary/Director

Jars Cider Ltd
Incorporated: 23 October 2018
Registered Office: Flat 4, 107 Finchampstead Road, Wokingham, Berks, RG41 2PF
Officers: Andrew James Carter [1992] Managing Director; Dr Sam Greatorex [1992] Technical Director; James William Maslin [1986] Director; Roy Edward Maslin [1961] Director

Jaspels Anglesey Craft Cider Ltd
Incorporated: 22 December 2017
Registered Office: Unit 3-4, Site 9, Amlwch Business Park, Amlwch, Anglesey, LL68 9BJ
Shareholders: Adrian Maurice Percival; Janet Iris Percival
Officers: Adrian Maurice Percival [1970] Director; Janet Iris Percival [1970] Director

Jordan's Car Review Ltd
Incorporated: 17 February 2015
Previous: Ruddy's Brewery & Bar Ltd
Registered Office: Flat 4, 19 Newerne Street, Lydney, Glos, GL15 5RA
Major Shareholder: Jordan Conall Smith
Officers: Jordan Smith [1992] Director

Kendal Brewery Ltd
Incorporated: 19 September 2017
Registered Office: Masons Yard 24, 22 Stramongate, Kendal, Cumbria, LA9 4BN
Shareholders: Jonathan Gillis Ritson; Darren Lincoln
Officers: Darren Lincoln [1968] Director/Joiner

Kent Cider Company Ltd
Incorporated: 4 March 2009 *Employees:* 3
Net Worth: £34,460 *Total Assets:* £89,380
Registered Office: King Arthurs Court, Maidstone Road, Charing, Ashford, Kent, TN27 0JS
Major Shareholder: Marcus Andrew Henderson
Officers: Mark Andrew Henderson [1968] Director

Kentish Maid Ltd
Incorporated: 14 September 2017
Registered Office: c/o Pembury Clarke Associates, Thames Innovation Centre, 2 Veridion Way, Erith, Kent, DA18 4AL
Major Shareholder: William Taylor
Officers: William Taylor [1986] Director/Railway Maintenance Operative

King Offa Ltd
Incorporated: 16 September 2015
Net Worth Deficit: £34,396 *Total Assets:* £26,521
Registered Office: Crowthers, 10 The Southend, Ledbury, Herefords, HR8 2EY
Major Shareholder: Theodore Tobias Bulmer
Officers: Theodore Tobias Bulmer [1986] Director/Cider Maker

Kingscote Winery Ltd
Incorporated: 6 July 2011
Net Worth Deficit: £10,718 *Total Assets:* £32,213
Registered Office: Pippens, Tickerage Lane, Blackboys, Uckfield, E Sussex, TN22 5LT
Shareholder: Anthony James Budd
Officers: Anthony James Budd [1968] Director; Christen Andrew Monge [1954] Director

The Kingston upon Hull Liqour Company Limited
Incorporated: 9 January 2017
Registered Office: 51 Chantry Way East, Swanland, North Ferriby, E Yorks, HU14 3QF
Officers: Iain Todd [1969] Director

Kingswood Cider Limited
Incorporated: 13 September 2013
Net Worth: £10,199 *Total Assets:* £25,722
Registered Office: 3 Lloyd Road, Broadstairs, Kent, CT10 1HY
Major Shareholder: Kevin John Newing
Officers: Kevin John Newing [1958] Director; Philippa Jo Watts [1964] Director

The Kinross Brewery Limited
Incorporated: 24 May 2016 *Employees:* 11
Net Worth: £169,482 *Total Assets:* £202,786
Registered Office: The Windlestrae, The Muirs, Kinross, KY13 8AS
Major Shareholder: James David Keith Montgomery
Officers: Gareth Derek Lee [1954] Director/Brewing Consultant; Anthony Gerard McGrath [1956] Director/Investor; Thomas Dodds Moffat [1967] Director/Marketing; James David Keith Montgomery [1957] Director/Hotelier; Alan John Roy [1951] Director; Daniel Christie Slater [1961] Director

L'Atypique Ltd
Incorporated: 12 September 2017
Registered Office: 11 Rosebery Court, London, EC1R 5HP
Major Shareholder: James Joseph Galbraith
Officers: James Joseph Galbraith [1980] Managing Director

The Lambswick Drinks Co Limited
Incorporated: 8 March 2013 *Employees:* 6
Net Worth Deficit: £42,139 *Total Assets:* £421,752
Registered Office: Oldfields Farm, Frith Common, Eardiston, Tenbury Wells, Worcs, WR15 8JX
Officers: Paul Anthony Albini [1958] Director; Martin John Churchward [1958] Director; Nicholas Edward James Davis [1965] Director; Geoffrey James Thompson [1956] Director; James Digby Thompson [1986] Director

Lamson Wine Company Limited
Incorporated: 6 March 2018
Registered Office: Health & Energy Drinks, Bridge House, 64-72 Mabgate, Leeds, LS9 7DZ
Major Shareholder: Robert (Elias) Wilson
Officers: Robert Wilson [1941] Director (CEO)

Lancashire Cider Limited
Incorporated: 15 December 2009 *Employees:* 2
Net Worth Deficit: £9,034 *Total Assets:* £11,181
Registered Office: Suite W11, 2nd Floor, Imex, 575-599 Maxted Road, Hemel Hempstead, Herts, HP2 7DX
Shareholders: Gareth Ellis; Simon Francis McDonald
Officers: Jane Hulland, Secretary; Gareth Ellis [1973] Director/Bar Manager; Simon Francis McDonald [1971] Director/Computer Programmer

Landshire Cider Ltd
Incorporated: 28 November 2013
Registered Office: New Barn Yard, Sandley, Gillingham, Dorset, SP8 5DZ
Major Shareholder: Oliver Reginald Tant
Officers: Oliver Reginald Tant [1961] Director/Chartered Accountant

Last Sign Brewing Company Ltd
Incorporated: 5 February 2018
Registered Office: 1 Bluebell Way, Worlingham, Beccles, Suffolk, NR34 7BT
Major Shareholder: Matthew James Caton
Officers: Matthew James Caton [1977] Director/Brewer

Laughing Ass Brewery Ltd
Incorporated: 20 February 2018
Registered Office: 49 Thorn Road, Hedon, E Yorks, HU12 8HN
Shareholders: Simon Paul North; Kelvin Hurd
Officers: Kelvin Hurd [1971] Director; Simon Paul North [1970] Director

Laycock Cider Ltd
Incorporated: 5 November 2018
Registered Office: 32 Prankerds Road, Milborne Port, Sherborne, Dorset, DT9 5BX
Major Shareholder: Angelo Ferrari
Officers: Angelo Ferrari [1971] Director

The Ledbury Cider and Juice Co. Limited
Incorporated: 17 September 2013 *Employees:* 2
Net Worth: £2,051 *Total Assets:* £49,300
Registered Office: The Old Kennels Farm, Bromyard Road, Ledbury, Herefords, HR8 1LG
Major Shareholder: Brian Maurice Wilce
Officers: Brian Maurice Wilce [1958] Director/Farmer; Peter Robert Wilce [1968] Business Development Director

Legiste Limited
Incorporated: 11 May 2000 *Employees:* 2
Net Worth: £8,540 *Total Assets:* £44,426
Registered Office: 257 Clifton Drive South, St Annes on Sea, Lytham St Annes, Lancs, FY8 1HW
Shareholders: Ian William Maynard; Fiona Jayne Dickson
Officers: Fiona Jayne Dickson [1965] Director/Solicitor

Levscreps Ltd
Incorporated: 3 November 2017
Registered Office: Flat 28, 4 Fleming Close, Maida Vale, London, W9 2AT
Major Shareholder: Leon Panton
Officers: Leon Panton [1984] Director/Social Worker; Levi Pryce [1994] Director/Cleaner

James Lewis Cider Ltd
Incorporated: 25 April 2018
Registered Office: c/o Clever Accounts Ltd, Brookfield Court, Selby Road, Leeds, LS25 1NB
Major Shareholder: James William Lewis
Officers: James William Lewis [1979] Director

Liberty Orchards Limited
Incorporated: 22 April 2010 *Employees:* 3
Net Worth Deficit: £16,554 *Total Assets:* £169,754
Registered Office: 14 Fairmont Terrace, Sherborne, Dorset, DT9 3JS
Officers: Robert Francis Imlach [1953] Director/Business Owner; Alison Jean Lemmey [1963] Director/Speech Therapist; Peter John Lemmey [1962] Director/Farmer; Victoria Morland [1965] Director/Publishing Manager

Lilley's Cider Limited
Incorporated: 12 May 2003 *Employees:* 35
Previous: Catering Leisure Services Ltd
Net Worth: £671,527 *Total Assets:* £2,567,968
Registered Office: Unit 7B, Handlemaker Road, Frome, Somerset, BA11 4RW
Shareholders: Christopher Stanley Alfred Lilley; Marc Lilley
Officers: Marc Lilley, Secretary; Christopher Stanley Alfred Lilley [1957] Director/Cater; Marc Lilley [1980] Director/Caterer

Lines Brew Co Ltd
Incorporated: 16 May 2016 *Employees:* 3
Net Worth: £8,518 *Total Assets:* £167,946
Registered Office: 37a Bridge Street, Usk, Monmouthshire, NP15 1BQ
Major Shareholder: Thomas George Newman
Officers: Amy Louisa Scarcella [1993] Director/Operations Manager

Lisnisky Cider Company Ltd
Incorporated: 10 October 2016
Net Worth Deficit: £812 *Total Assets:* £4,944
Registered Office: 49 The Slopes, Portadown, Craigavon, Co Armagh, BT63 5NT
Major Shareholder: Nikolas Jolmes
Officers: Nikolas Jolmes [1978] Director

Little Teapot Ltd
Incorporated: 18 September 2018
Registered Office: 5 Kingsley Grove, Audenshaw, Manchester, M34 5GT
Major Shareholder: James Robert Whewell
Officers: James Robert Whewell [1980] Director

Little Wolf Brewing Limited
Incorporated: 23 April 2018
Registered Office: 5 Bangholm Park, Edinburgh, EH5 3BA
Major Shareholder: Sean Woelfell Fleming
Officers: Sean Woelfell Fleming [1989] Director/Brewer

The London Beer Company Limited
Incorporated: 7 August 1992
Net Worth: £146,296 *Total Assets:* £438,913
Registered Office: Suite 215, Waterhouse Business Centre, Cromar Way, Chelmsford, Essex, CM1 2QE
Major Shareholder: Martin Kemp
Officers: Martin Kemp, Secretary/Business Executive; Martin Kemp [1957] Director/Business Executive

London Cider Company Ltd
Incorporated: 6 November 2013
Registered Office: 1 Palmerston Park, Tiverton, Devon, EX16 5PG
Major Shareholder: Kieran Michael Aylward
Officers: Kieran Aylward [1982] Director/Brewer

The Long Ashton Cider Company Limited
Incorporated: 11 February 2004
Registered Office: Cox's Green, Wrington, Bristol, BS40 5PA
Parent: Butcombe Brewing Company Limited
Officers: Richard Stuart Grainger [1960] Director; Timothy Hubert [1962] Commercial Director; Nigel Richard Osborne [1966] Director

Long Meadow Cider Ltd
Incorporated: 23 June 2014 *Employees:* 1
Net Worth: £6,850 *Total Assets:* £119,767
Registered Office: 87 Loughgall Road, Portadown, Craigavon, Co Armagh, BT62 4EG
Major Shareholder: Patrick McKeever
Officers: Patrick McKeever [1967] Director/Apple Grower [Irish]

Lost Boys Brewery Ltd
Incorporated: 30 January 2017
Net Worth: £4 *Total Assets:* £4
Registered Office: Tillbrook Cottage, 153b High Street, London Colney, St Albans, Herts, AL2 1RP
Officers: Mark Hamilton Howarth, Secretary; Jonathan Hamilton Howarth [1993] Director/Warehouse Assistant; Joshua James Kitt [1994] Director/Carpenter; Jordan Manfre [1993] Director/Community Support Officer; George Sanderson [1993] Director/Recruitment Consultant

The Lovely Cider Company Limited
Incorporated: 26 September 2011
Registered Office: The Grange, Woodhouses, Yoxall, Burton on Trent, Staffs, DE13 8NP
Major Shareholder: James Scott Williams
Officers: James Scott Williams [1962] Director

Loxley Cider Limited
Incorporated: 25 October 2017
Registered Office: The Barn, Hockerwood Park, Hockerwood Lane, Southwell, Notts, NG25 0PZ
Major Shareholder: James Parker
Officers: James Parker [1992] Director; Wayne Russell Stevens [1957] Director

Ludlow Vineyard Limited
Incorporated: 17 November 2003
Registered Office: Wainbridge House, Clee St Margaret, Craven Arms, Salop, SY7 9DT
Shareholders: Barbara Eileen Hardingham; Barbara Eileen Hardingham; Michael John Hardingham
Officers: Michael John Hardingham, Secretary/Administrator; Barbara Eileen Hardingham [1939] Director/Administrator; Michael John Hardingham [1956] Director/Administrator

Luminati Wine Limited
Incorporated: 21 March 2018
Registered Office: 221B Nantwich Road, Crewe, Cheshire, CW2 6DA
Major Shareholder: Lucifer Fawcett
Officers: Lucifer Fawcett [1989] Director

Lyme Bay Cider Company Limited
Incorporated: 27 August 1993
Net Worth: £2,744,107 *Total Assets:* £5,223,414
Registered Office: The Lyme Bay Winery, Shute, Seaton Junction, Axminster, Devon, EX13 7PW
Parent: Ball Capital Investment Limited
Officers: Andrew Robert Beasley, Secretary; Keith Michael Ball [1969] Director; Andrew Robert Beasley [1967] Director; James Lawrence Lambert [1981] Director

Lyme Bay Winery Limited
Incorporated: 21 August 2008
Net Worth: £600,034 *Total Assets:* £600,034
Registered Office: The Lyme Bay Winery, Shute, Seaton Junction, Axminster, Devon, EX13 7PW
Parent: Ball Capital Investment Limited
Officers: Andrew Robert Beasley, Secretary; Keith Michael Ball [1969] Director; Andrew Robert Beasley [1967] Director; James Lawrence Lambert [1981] Director

Lyne Down Organics Limited
Incorporated: 19 July 2016
Net Worth Deficit: £37,651 *Total Assets:* £20,077
Registered Office: The Cider Barn, Lyne Down, Much Marcle, Ledbury, Herefords, HR8 2NT
Shareholders: Ian Scott John Marshall; Sabine Claire Darrall
Officers: Sabine Claire Darrall [1965] Director; Ian Scott John Marshall [1964] Director

Mabinogion Mead Company Limited
Incorporated: 27 November 2014
Net Worth Deficit: £11,494 *Total Assets:* £45,688
Registered Office: 4 Uskside Cottages, Caerleon, Newport, NP18 1BP
Major Shareholder: Thomas George Newman
Officers: Thomas George Newman, Secretary; Thomas George Newman [1975] Director

Mac Ivors Cider Co. Limited
Incorporated: 28 March 2013
Net Worth: £204,043 *Total Assets:* £714,521
Registered Office: 65a Ardress Road, Portadown, Craigavon, Co Armagh, BT62 1SQ
Major Shareholder: Gregory MacNeice
Officers: Gregory MacNeice [1972] Director [Irish]

The Mad Yank Brewery Ltd
Incorporated: 15 December 2017
Registered Office: Tad Accountancy Services, 106 The Avenue, Pinner, Middlesex, HA5 5BJ
Shareholders: Grant Kelly Graeber; Larissa Michelle Graeber
Officers: Grant Kelly Graeber [1978] Director/Chief Executive [American]; Larissa Michelle Graeber [1979] Director/Chief Executive [German]

Magners GB Limited
Incorporated: 1 November 2009 *Employees:* 2
Net Worth: £37,743,000 *Total Assets:* £169,904,000
Registered Office: Ashford House, Grenadier Road, Exeter, Devon, EX1 3LH
Parent: C & C Holdings (NI) Limited
Officers: Stephen Glancey [1960] Director; Thomas Michael McCusker [1957] Managing Director; Andrea Pozzi [1971] Managing Director

The Malmesbury Cider Company Ltd
Incorporated: 29 February 2016
Net Worth: £100 *Total Assets:* £100
Registered Office: 21 Oxford Street, Malmesbury, Wilts, SN16 9AX
Major Shareholder: Robert Beattie
Officers: Robert Beattie [1965] Director

Malton Cider Ltd
Incorporated: 10 May 2018
Registered Office: Coach House, Firby, York, YO60 7LH
Major Shareholder: Professor Alan William Murray
Officers: Professor Alan William Murray [1950] Director/Professor

Manmax Ltd
Incorporated: 23 July 2018
Registered Office: Suite 6, First Floor, Wordsworth Mill, Wordsworth Street, Bolton, Lancs, BL1 3ND
Major Shareholder: Paul Noble
Officers: Josephine Lipao [1969] Director [Filipino]

Marches Bottling and Packaging Limited
Incorporated: 3 August 2016 *Employees:* 6
Net Worth Deficit: £328,617 *Total Assets:* £871,052
Registered Office: 22 Farley Road, Malvern, Worcs, WR14 1NF
Shareholders: Susan Jeanette Vaughan; Robert James Hancocks; Robert James Hancocks
Officers: Darren Morris, Secretary; Robert James Hancocks [1967] Director; Darren John Morris [1968] Director; Chistopher James Palmes [1968] Operations Director; Susan Jeanette Vaughan [1962] Director

Marley and Barley Ltd
Incorporated: 23 February 2016
Registered Office: Clayton Farm, Church Lane, Peasmarsh, Rye, E Sussex, TN31 6XS
Shareholders: Stephen Charles Reeve; Jaqueline Reeve
Officers: Jaqueline Reeve [1947] Director/Farmer; Stephen Charles Reeve [1978] Director/Farmer

Marourde Limited
Incorporated: 17 January 2017
Registered Office: Suite 5, 10 Churchill Square, West Malling, Kent, ME19 4YU
Major Shareholder: Evelyn George William Boscawen
Officers: Evelyn George William Boscawen [1979] Director

Marron (Lincoln) Ltd
Incorporated: 9 May 2011
Net Worth Deficit: £56,811 *Total Assets:* £23,794
Registered Office: 9 Broadbeck, Waddingham, Lincoln, DN21 4TH
Shareholders: Ronald Edgar; Margaret Edgar
Officers: Margaret Edgar [1951] Director/Retired; Ronald Edgar [1949] Director/Sales Person

Marsh Barton Farm Cyder Limited
Incorporated: 1 November 1989 *Employees:* 5
Previous: Green Valley Cyder Limited
Net Worth: £110,889 *Total Assets:* £123,735
Registered Office: Darts Farm, Clyst St George, Exeter, Devon, EX3 0QH
Major Shareholder: Christopher John Coles
Officers: Nicholas William Pring, Secretary; Dr Christopher John Coles [1944] Managing Director; Elzbieta Eugenia Coles [1947] Director/Retired; Nicholas William Pring [1949] Operations Director

L. McCoy Drinks Limited
Incorporated: 27 October 2016 *Employees:* 1
Net Worth Deficit: £8,394 *Total Assets:* £12,080
Registered Office: Waterworks House, Pluckley Road, Charing, Ashford, Kent, TN27 0AH
Officers: Luke Laurence McCoy [1991] Director

The Meanwood Brewery Ltd
Incorporated: 2 December 2016 *Employees:* 2
Net Worth Deficit: £5,977 *Total Assets:* £4,372
Registered Office: 8a Stonegate Road, Meanwood, Leeds, LS6 4YH
Shareholders: Graeme Phillips; Barry Jon Phillips
Officers: Barry Jon Phillips [1984] Director/Advisor; Graeme Phillips [1981] Director

Medland Manor Vineyard Ltd.
Incorporated: 15 October 2018
Registered Office: Medland Manor, Cheriton Bishop, Exeter, EX6 6HE
Major Shareholder: Einar Finn Hafstad
Officers: Einar Finn Hafstad [1959] Managing Director

Medlar Management Limited
Incorporated: 15 February 2010 *Employees:* 3
Net Worth: £292,227 *Total Assets:* £303,026
Registered Office: The Manor House, Leathley Lane, Leathley, Otley, W Yorks, LS21 2JU
Shareholders: Ann Buxton; Edward John Buxton
Officers: Ann Buxton [1956] Director/Consultant Histopathologist; Edward John Buxton [1956] Director/Retired Surgeon; Imogen Sarah Clay [1986] Director/Teacher

Meon Valley Cider Ltd
Incorporated: 23 April 2015
Net Worth Deficit: £28,141 *Total Assets:* £50,941
Registered Office: Marldell House, Church Lane, West Meon, Hants, GU32 1JP
Shareholders: Nigel Douglas Hamilton Johnson; Charlotte Frances Johnson
Officers: Charlotte Johnson, Secretary; Charlotte Frances Johnson [1959] Director; Nigel Douglas Hamilton Johnson [1957] Director

Merrydown PLC
Incorporated: 22 November 1946 *Employees:* 1
Net Worth: £26,722,968 *Total Assets:* £51,247,252
Registered Office: 5230 Valiant Court, Delta Way, Brockworth, Gloucester, GL3 4FE
Parent: SHS Group Ltd
Officers: Arthur William Richmond, Secretary; Elaine Birchall [1966] Director [Irish]; Arthur William Richmond [1966] Director/Accountant; Joseph Sloan [1946] Director/Group Chairman

Missing Link Brewing Ltd
Incorporated: 2 May 2017 *Employees:* 3
Net Worth Deficit: £12,286 *Total Assets:* £11,439
Registered Office: Suite 6, 141-143 South Road, Haywards Heath, W Sussex, RH16 4LZ
Major Shareholder: Jeremy Mark Cook
Officers: Jeremy Mark Cook [1974] Director/Business Owner

Monkey Shed Estate Brewing Co Ltd
Incorporated: 9 June 2017
Registered Office: Beaumont, Woodbury Lane, Norton, Worcester, WR5 2PT
Major Shareholder: Richard Bakewell Phillips
Officers: Richard Bakewell Phillips [1966] Director/Farmer

Moss Cider Limited
Incorporated: 20 February 2012
Net Worth: £3,623 *Total Assets:* £38,295
Registered Office: 12 Jordan Street, Liverpool, L1 0BP
Major Shareholder: Joseph Paul Weeks
Officers: Joseph Paul Weeks [1973] Director

H.Mount & Sons Limited
Incorporated: 8 November 1946 *Employees:* 7
Net Worth: £4,394,275 *Total Assets:* £5,440,523
Registered Office: Woolton Farm, Bekesbourne, Canterbury, Kent, CT4 5EA
Major Shareholder: Mark Donald Crichton Mount
Officers: Mark Donald Crichton Mount, Secretary; Camilla Lucy Mount [1984] Director; Mark Donald Crichton Mount [1957] Managing Director; Rosemary Helen Mount [1958] Director; Sam Alexander Mount [1986] Director/Project Manager

Mount Bank Farm Limited
Incorporated: 20 February 2015 *Employees:* 5
Net Worth: £133,270 *Total Assets:* £206,694
Registered Office: Mount Bank Farm, Northallerton, N Yorks, DL6 2TE
Shareholders: Evan Peter Thompson; Stacey Thompson
Officers: Stacey Thompson, Secretary; Evan Peter Thompson [1980] Director

Mr. Whitehead's Cider Company Ltd
Incorporated: 9 October 2003 *Employees:* 9
Net Worth: £156,879 *Total Assets:* £474,358
Registered Office: Windmill Farm, Colemore Lane, Colemore, Alton, Hants, GU34 3PY
Major Shareholder: Alexander Whitehead
Officers: Alexander Whitehead, Secretary/Cidermaker/Draughtsman/Engineer; Robert Charles Maltby [1945] Director/Engineer; Alexander Whitehead [1971] Director/Cidermaker/Draughtsman/Engineer

Mr. Whitehead's Drinks Company Ltd.
Incorporated: 30 January 2012
Registered Office: Windmill Farm, Colemore Lane, Colemore, Alton, Hants, GU34 3PY
Major Shareholder: Alexander Whitehead
Officers: Alexander Whitehead [1971] Director/Drinks Producer

Nada General Trading Ltd
Incorporated: 1 February 2019
Registered Office: 20-22 Wenlock Road, London, N1 7GU
Major Shareholder: Eman Nasser Sabah Alnasser Alsabah
Officers: Eman Nasser Sabah Alnasser Alsabah [1964] Director [Kuwaiti]

Napton Cidery Limited
Incorporated: 24 February 2016
Net Worth Deficit: £70,068 *Total Assets:* £90,495
Registered Office: Holroyd House Farm, Napton, Southam, Warwicks, CV47 8NY
Major Shareholder: Jolyon Charles Olivier
Officers: Charlotte Olivier [1982] Director; Jolyon Charles Olivier [1986] Director

Neptune SA Ltd
Incorporated: 12 March 2018
Registered Office: Mays Grove Cottage, Mays Lane, Dedham, Colchester, Essex, CO7 6EW
Officers: Antanas Sadauskas [1965] Director [Lithuanian]

New Forest Cider Limited
Incorporated: 23 March 2010 *Employees:* 28
Net Worth: £4 *Total Assets:* £922,869
Registered Office: Suite 2b, Lynes House, Lynes Lane, High Street, Ringwood, Hants, BH24 1BT
Officers: Sally Anne Topp, Secretary; Barry John Chissell Topp [1948] Director; James Herbert Topp [1973] Director; John William Henry Topp [1971] Director; Mary Louise Topp [1983] Director; Sally Anne Topp [1974] Director; Susan Daphne Topp [1950] Director

The New Union Brewing Company Limited
Incorporated: 31 January 2019
Registered Office: 159 Stricklandgate, Kendal, Cumbria, LA9 4RF
Officers: Martin James Boyd [1968] Director/Architectural Technician; Philip Lawrence John Walker [1986] Director/Publican

Nightingale Cider Company Limited
Incorporated: 16 June 2017 *Employees:* 2
Net Worth Deficit: £11,254 *Total Assets:* £60,279
Registered Office: Park Farm Barn, Brabourne Lees, Ashford, Kent, TN25 6RG
Shareholders: Peter Alan Nightingale; Samuel Patrick Nightingale
Officers: Peter Alan Nightingale [1949] Director/Fruit Farmer; Samuel Patrick Nightingale [1981] Director/Farmer & Cider Maker

Noahs Estate Ltd
Incorporated: 8 March 2018
Registered Office: 36 Park Lane, Wilberfoss, York, YO41 5PW
Major Shareholder: Jonathan Atkin
Officers: Jonathan Atkin [1984] Director/Businessman

Noddy's Cider Ltd
Incorporated: 31 July 2018
Registered Office: 5 Dale Avenue, Weymouth, Dorset, DT4 7RB
Shareholders: Nigel Desmond Jelfs; Penelope Sue Jelfs
Officers: Nigel Desmond Jelfs [1956] Director/Retailer

North Coast Cider Company Limited
Incorporated: 30 September 2013
Net Worth Deficit: £35,940 *Total Assets:* £46,046
Registered Office: Norton Barton Farm, Launcells, Bude, Cornwall, EX23 9LG
Shareholder: Richard William Harding
Officers: Fionagh Mason Harding [1962] Director/Farmer; Richard William Harding [1962] Director/Entrepreneur

The Not Real Wine Company Ltd
Incorporated: 3 September 2018
Registered Office: 95 Linton Heath, Linton, Swadlincote, Derbys, DE12 6PD
Major Shareholder: Christopher Philip Hart
Officers: Christopher Philip Hart [1975] Director/Forest Ranger

Oast Ventures Limited
Incorporated: 8 May 2017
Registered Office: Oast Cottage, Grange Hill, Plaxtol, Sevenoaks, Kent, TN15 0RG
Major Shareholder: Natalie Nagaoka Newton
Officers: Natalie Nagaoka Newton [1990] Director

Old Chads Orchard Ltd
Incorporated: 19 June 2014
Net Worth: £11,109 *Total Assets:* £33,729
Registered Office: 62 Well Street, Malpas, Cheshire, SY14 8QH
Major Shareholder: Stephen Charles Richard Wright
Officers: Stephen Charles Richard Wright [1974] Director

Old Town Brewery Ltd.
Incorporated: 8 April 2013
Net Worth Deficit: £9,346 *Total Assets:* £9,611
Registered Office: 25 Goddard Avenue, Swindon, Wilts, SN1 4HR
Major Shareholder: David Michael Bugg
Officers: Clare Bugg, Secretary; David Michael Bugg [1980] Director/Head Brewer

Old Tree Brewery Ltd
Incorporated: 6 February 2018
Registered Office: Yacht Werks, 28-29 Richmond Place, Brighton, BN2 9NA
Major Shareholder: Thomas Charles Averell Daniell
Officers: Harold Abel [1992] Director; Thomas Charles Averell Daniell [1987] Director; Eve Beryl Jones [1991] Director and Company Secretary; Matthew Stuart Nash [1981] Director

Olde Mill Ltd
Incorporated: 18 February 2014
Net Worth Deficit: £19,263 *Total Assets:* £25,614
Registered Office: Tax Shop, 9 High Street, Wellington, Somerset, TA21 8QT
Shareholder: Kieran Michael Aylward
Officers: Kieran Aylward [1982] Director

Oliver's Cider and Perry Limited
Incorporated: 9 February 2009
Net Worth: £6,596 *Total Assets:* £186,570
Registered Office: Stanksbridge, Ocle Pychard, Herefords, HR1 3RE
Major Shareholder: Thomas Richard Oliver
Officers: Thomas Richard Oliver [1956] Director/Cidermaker

One Swan Ltd
Incorporated: 23 February 2018
Registered Office: 29 Josephine Avenue, Limavady, Co Londonderry, BT49 9BA
Major Shareholder: Conor McKay
Officers: Lauren Hutton, Secretary; Conor McKay [1997] Director/Consultancy [Irish]

Onefolks Ltd
Incorporated: 24 May 2018
Registered Office: Office 3, 146-148 Bury Old Road, Whitefield, Manchester, M45 6AT
Shareholders: Sarah Monica Sebastian; Leanne Michelle Whitehead
Officers: Sarah Monica Sebastian [1984] Director [Filipino]

Orchard Origins C.I.C.
Incorporated: 15 December 2014
Registered Office: Queenswood Country Park, Dinmore Hill, Leominster, Herefords, HR6 0PY
Parent: Herefordshire Wildlife Trust
Officers: Peter James Ford [1955] Director/Retired; Laurence John Green [1977] Director/Manager; Brian Peter Robert Hurrell [1943] Director; Sally Jane Pike [1957] Director; Adrian Wilcox [1951] Director/Social Work

The Orchard Pig Ltd
Incorporated: 5 January 2007 *Employees:* 21
Net Worth: £1,284,882 *Total Assets:* £3,199,530
Registered Office: West Bradley Orchards, West Bradley, Glastonbury, Somerset, BA6 8LT
Parent: C & C Holdings (NI) Limited
Officers: Jason James Sproule Ash [1974] Director; Andrea Pozzi [1971] Director

Organic Country Drinks Ltd
Incorporated: 29 March 2005
Net Worth Deficit: £688 *Total Assets:* £1,449
Registered Office: Sportsman Farm, St Michaels, Tenterden, Kent, TN30 6SY
Shareholders: William Roy Cook; Irma Cook
Officers: Richard Michael Marney, Secretary; Irma Cook [1957] Director/Administrator; William Roy Cook [1946] Director/Wine Producer

The Orgasmic Cider Co. Ltd
Incorporated: 17 May 2002 *Employees:* 3
Net Worth: £43,406 *Total Assets:* £69,786
Registered Office: West Lodge, Rainbow Street, Leominster, Herefords, HR6 8DQ
Shareholders: Stephen Denis Layton; William Andrew Layton
Officers: Gillian Layton, Secretary; Claire Layton [1959] Director; Stephen Denis Layton [1960] Director/Farmer; William Andrew Layton [1957] Director/Farmer

The UK Cider Industry

Ostlers Cider Mill Limited
Incorporated: 9 November 2004
Registered Office: Ostlers Cider Mill, Northleigh Hill, Goodleigh, Barnstaple, Devon, EX32 7NR
Shareholders: Rebekah Sasha Paterson; Peter Walden Hartnoll
Officers: Peter Walden Hartnoll [1940] Director/Cider Retailer; Rebekah Sasha Paterson [1973] Director/Cider Vinegar Retailer

Overtone Brewing Ltd
Incorporated: 6 February 2017
Net Worth Deficit: £56,480 *Total Assets:* £112,528
Registered Office: Unit 19 Halley Street, New Albion Industrial Estate, Glasgow, G13 4DJ
Major Shareholder: Bowei Wang
Officers: Bowei Wang [1982] Director/Brewer

Thomas Paine Brewery Limited
Incorporated: 1 November 2016
Registered Office: Woodview, Hanby Lane, Welton-le-Marsh, Lincs, PE23 5TH
Officers: Kerry Lancaster, Secretary; David Albert Lancaster [1953] Director/Industrial Designer

Parsonage Farm (Croscombe) Ltd
Incorporated: 5 January 2015
Net Worth: £3,865 *Total Assets:* £12,232
Registered Office: Parsonage Farm, Croscombe, Wells, Somerset, BA5 3QN
Officers: James Neil Morris [1970] Director/Consultant; Nicola Jane Morris [1976] Director/Management Consultant

Peak Ciders Limited
Incorporated: 12 June 2015
Registered Office: Alexandra House, Queen Street, Leek, Staffs, ST13 6LP
Shareholders: Adrian Corke; Beth Nadine Simpson
Officers: Beth Nadine Simpson, Secretary; Adrian Corke [1965] Director; Beth Nadine Simpson [1965] Director

Pearsons Ciderworks Ltd
Incorporated: 29 January 2013 *Employees:* 2
Net Worth: £17,754 *Total Assets:* £268,098
Registered Office: Unit 3 Newtown Trading Estate, Northway Lane, Tewkesbury, Glos, GL20 8JG
Shareholder: Michael Justin Pearson
Officers: Michael Justin Pearson [1969] Director

The Peasmarsh Cider Company Limited
Incorporated: 25 July 2017
Net Worth: £372 *Total Assets:* £8,463
Registered Office: Clayton Farm, Church Lane, Peasmarsh, Rye, E Sussex, TN31 6XS
Officers: Stephen Charles Reeve [1978] Director; Benjamin James Walgate [1979] Director

Pembrokeshire Cider Limited
Incorporated: 24 March 2016
Net Worth: £15,553 *Total Assets:* £31,168
Registered Office: 6 Commons Road, Pembroke, SA71 4EB
Shareholders: David Michael Halsted; Jonathan Ashley Ryan; Christopher Gordon Scourfield
Officers: David Michael Halsted [1959] Director; Jonathan Ashley Ryan [1967] Director

Pennine Cider Limited
Incorporated: 11 December 2017
Net Worth Deficit: £2,609 *Total Assets:* £391
Registered Office: 17 Bobbin Close, Golcar, Huddersfield, W Yorks, HD7 4DQ
Major Shareholder: David Hinchliffe
Officers: David Hinchliffe [1970] Director

Penton Park Brewery Limited
Incorporated: 15 April 2014 *Employees:* 2
Previous: Pentafra Limited
Net Worth: £27 *Total Assets:* £153,757
Registered Office: Midland House, 2 Poole Road, Bournemouth, BH2 5QY
Shareholders: Danielle Marie Rolfe; Guy William Rolfe
Officers: Danielle Marie Rolfe [1981] Director/Self Employed; Guy William Rolfe [1981] Director/Self Employed

Perry's Cider Limited
Incorporated: 6 June 2012 *Employees:* 16
Net Worth: £221,124 *Total Assets:* £875,308
Registered Office: The Cider Mills, Dowlish Wake, Ilminster, Somerset, TA19 0NY
Shareholder: Jonathan Henry Perry
Officers: Andrew Perry [1954] Director/Estate Agent; George Henry John Perry [1981] Director/Manager; Jonathan Henry Perry [1950] Director/Chartered Accountant

Pickers Cider Limited
Incorporated: 15 January 2018
Registered Office: Kimberley Lodge, Furnace Lane, Broad Oak, Rye, E Sussex, TN31 6ES
Major Shareholder: Harry Pickering
Officers: Harry Pickering [1987] Director/Cider Maker

Pilango Limited
Incorporated: 24 June 2016 *Employees:* 1
Net Worth Deficit: £25,550 *Total Assets:* £28,073
Registered Office: Railway Arch 10, Munster Road, Fulham, London, SW6 4RY
Major Shareholder: Wiktor Edward Zygmunt Zasadzki
Officers: Wiktor Edward Zygmunt Zasadzki [1982] Director

Pips Cider Limited
Incorporated: 16 August 2010
Net Worth Deficit: £91 *Total Assets:* £11,476
Registered Office: Mill Cottage, Dorstone, Hereford, HR3 6BN
Major Shareholder: Diane Susan Phillips
Officers: Alistair David Phillips [1985] Production Director; Diane Susan Phillips [1960] Director/Housewife

Polaners Ltd
Incorporated: 20 August 2018
Registered Office: 9 Knowl Street, Oldham, Lancs, OL8 3RG
Major Shareholder: Jodie McClelland
Officers: Jodie McClelland [1985] Director/Consultant

Polecat Cider Limited
Incorporated: 24 October 2018
Registered Office: 3 Lisle Close, Newbury, Berks, RG14 1PT
Major Shareholder: Jonathan Matthew Fitch
Officers: Jonathan Matthew Fitch [1975] Director/Teacher

Polgoon Vineyard Ltd
Incorporated: 26 November 2018
Registered Office: Polgoon Farmhouse, Polgoon Farm, Rosehill, Penzance, Cornwall, TR20 8TE
Shareholders: John Paul Coulson; Kim Marie Coulson
Officers: John Paul Coulson [1962] Director/Winemaker

Pomona Orchards Ltd
Incorporated: 20 April 2017
Net Worth Deficit: £2,531 *Total Assets:* £1,965
Registered Office: 29 New Road, Banbridge, Co Down, BT32 4EA
Shareholders: Richard Parton; Lynda Parton
Officers: Lynda Parton [1982] Director/Music Teacher; Mr Richard Parton [1982] Director/Music Teacher

The Portsmouth Distillery Company Limited
Incorporated: 4 July 2018
Registered Office: Coastguard Casemate, Fort Cumberland, Fort Cumberland Road, Southsea, Hants, PO4 9LD
Parent: The Rum Club Ltd
Officers: Giles Thomas Collighan [1968] Director/Consultant; Vincent Robert Amos Noyce [1968] Director/Distiller

Primeflow Limited
Incorporated: 27 May 2002 *Employees:* 1
Net Worth Deficit: £31,995 *Total Assets:* £128,051
Registered Office: Newton Court Farm, Newton, Leominster, Herefords, HR6 0PF
Major Shareholder: Paul Benjamin Stephens
Officers: Paul Benjamin Stephens, Secretary; Paul Benjamin Stephens [1970] Director/Cider Manufacturer

Proasset Limited
Incorporated: 21 May 2002
Net Worth: £2,104 *Total Assets:* £34,875
Registered Office: 85 Deardengate, Haslingden, Rossendale, Lancs, BB4 5SN
Major Shareholder: Anita Thorne
Officers: Anita Thorne [1972] Director

The Purbeck Cider Company Limited
Incorporated: 4 November 2009 *Employees:* 6
Net Worth Deficit: £39,452 *Total Assets:* £411,010
Registered Office: Midland House, 2 Poole Road, Bournemouth, BH2 5QY
Major Shareholder: Joseph Mark Hartle
Officers: Joesph Hartle [1986] Director/Farmer

Puxted Cider Limited
Incorporated: 11 October 2017
Registered Office: Puxted Orchard, Brenchley Road, Brenchley, Tonbridge, Kent, TN12 7PB
Parent: Bocs and Docs Limited
Officers: Katherine Bunyan [1979] Director; Martin John Bunyan [1974] Director

The Radnage Cider Company Ltd
Incorporated: 19 December 2011
Net Worth: £1,659 *Total Assets:* £3,723
Registered Office: Mulberry House, 4 Pound Lane, Marlow, Bucks, SL7 2AQ
Shareholder: Michelle Goldsmith
Officers: Michael Barlow, Secretary; Michelle Goldsmith [1978] Director; John Scales [1982] Director

Ralph's Cider Ltd
Incorporated: 20 June 2013
Net Worth: £5,257 *Total Assets:* £37,385
Registered Office: Old Badland, New Radnor, Presteigne, Powys, LD8 2TG
Shareholders: Ralph David James Owen; Mary Elizabeth Owen
Officers: Ralph David James Owen [1953] Director/Cider Maker

The Regal Rogue Group UK Limited
Incorporated: 21 May 2014 *Employees:* 2
Net Worth Deficit: £452,974 *Total Assets:* £100,893
Registered Office: One Bell Lane, Lewes, E Sussex, BN7 1JU
Major Shareholder: Mark Jonathan Ward
Officers: Mark Jonathan Ward [1977] Director

Renegade Wines Limited
Incorporated: 18 May 2016
Registered Office: 95 Longton Avenue, Sydenham, London, SE26 6RF
Shareholders: Brendan Thomson; Frank Richard Neal
Officers: Frank Richard Neal [1959] Director; Brendan Thomson [1989] Director

Revenant Cider Limited
Incorporated: 18 January 2016
Net Worth Deficit: £4,545 *Total Assets:* £11,791
Registered Office: 25 Kinsale Road, London, SE15 4HJ
Officers: George Foster [1979] Director; Paul Gudonis [1976] Director; Philip Josiah Harding [1978] Director/Consultant; Lawrence Jewkes [1987] Director; James Alexander Sandrini [1984] Director/Consultant; Richard Williams [1985] Director [New Zealander]

Robinsons Cider Limited
Incorporated: 24 August 2010 *Employees:* 4
Net Worth: £175,258 *Total Assets:* £396,674
Registered Office: Woodhampton House, Little Hereford, Ludlow, Salop, SY8 4LR
Parent: The Robinsons Group of Companies Limited
Officers: Susan Kinloch Robinson, Secretary; Angus Charles Robinson [1987] Director; Nicholas Robert John Robinson [1985] Director; Robert Charles Christian Robinson [1955] Director; Susan Kinloch Robinson [1953] Director

Rock Hill Cider Company Limited
Incorporated: 4 July 2018
Registered Office: 53 Amwell Street, London, EC1R 1UR
Shareholders: Charlotte Louise Clifton Robinson; Dickon Hugh Wheelwright Robinson
Officers: Charlotte Louise Clifton Robinson [1947] Director/Bookseller/Cider Maker; Dickon Hugh Wheelwright Robinson [1945] Director/Regeneration Consultant/Cider Maker

Ross-on-Wye Cider & Perry Company Limited
Incorporated: 20 February 2003 *Employees:* 7
Net Worth: £20,676 *Total Assets:* £108,212
Registered Office: Broome Farm, Peterstow, Ross on Wye, Herefords, HR9 6QG
Officers: Cindy Smith, Secretary; Albert James Johnson [1993] Director/Business Executive; Michael James Johnson [1952] Director/Farmer; Cindy Smith [1957] Director/Accountant

The Rutland Cider Company Limited
Incorporated: 5 August 2016
Registered Office: 110 Regent Road, Leicester, LE1 7LT
Parent: Spidercrab Limited
Officers: Peter David Atkinson [1972] Director; William Anthony Davis [1974] Director

Sadler-Wilson & Read Ltd
Incorporated: 9 November 2018
Registered Office: 1 Marine Drive, Hornsea, E Yorks, HU18 1NJ
Shareholders: Harry George Read; Finlay Sadler-Wilson
Officers: Harry George Read [1995] Director/Retailer; Finlay Sadler-Wilson [1996] Director/Student

Saint Patricks Ltd
Incorporated: 15 February 2018
Registered Office: 20-22 Wenlock Road, London, N1 7GU
Major Shareholder: Patrick Hayden
Officers: Patrick Hayden [1987] Director/Founder

Salcombe Cider Company Ltd
Incorporated: 5 December 2016
Registered Office: Holwell Farm, South Huish, Kingsbridge, Devon, TQ7 3EQ
Major Shareholder: Duncan Walker Burnett
Officers: Duncan Walker Burnett [1986] Director/Cider Maker

Samba Cidra Ltd
Incorporated: 20 July 2016
Net Worth: £550 *Total Assets:* £550
Registered Office: 42 Ivel Gardens, Biggleswade, Beds, SG18 0AN
Major Shareholder: George Pires Higginson
Officers: George Pires Higginson [1995] Director; Phoebe Puttock [1996] Director/Student

Sandford Orchards Limited
Incorporated: 22 January 2016 *Employees:* 12
Net Worth: £149,443 *Total Assets:* £1,345,649
Registered Office: Haines Watts Crediton, Parliament Square, Parliament Street, Crediton, Devon, EX17 2AW
Major Shareholder: William Butterfield
Officers: William Butterfield [1977] Director/Cider Maker

Saxby Farms Limited
Incorporated: 30 May 2013 *Employees:* 2
Net Worth Deficit: £54,729 *Total Assets:* £274,484
Registered Office: The Haunches, Home Farm, Abbots Ripton, Huntingdon, Cambs, PE28 2LD
Shareholders: Philip John Saxby; Amanda Jane Saxby
Officers: Amanda Jane Saxby [1970] Director/Farmer; Philip John Saxby [1968] Director/Farmer

Scott's Irish Whisky Ltd
Incorporated: 9 November 2017
Registered Office: 15 Railway Road, Belcoo, Co Fermanagh, BT93 4EL
Major Shareholder: Conal Treacy
Officers: Conal Treacy [1967] Director

Scrumpy Wasp Limited
Incorporated: 16 September 2011
Net Worth Deficit: £194,289 *Total Assets:* £97,664
Registered Office: Rose Dean Farm, Mark Lane, East Markham, Newark, Notts, NG22 0QU
Shareholders: Timothy Paul Needham; Leanda Daphne Needham
Officers: Leanda Daphne Needham [1971] Director/P.A; Timothy Paul Needham [1960] Director/Brewer

Secret Orchard Cider Ltd
Incorporated: 30 November 2012
Net Worth: £6,793 *Total Assets:* £9,803
Registered Office: Nettle Combe Studios, Nettlecombe, Williton, Taunton, Somerset, TA4 4HS
Major Shareholder: Joe Heley
Officers: Joseph Peter Heley [1984] Director; Todd Matthew Studley [1984] Director/Lecturer

Sephylia Ltd
Incorporated: 20 August 2018
Registered Office: 38 Elysian Street, Openshaw, Manchester, M11 2GH
Major Shareholder: Sarah Minchella
Officers: Sarah Minchella [1992] Director/Consultant

Severn Cider Ltd
Incorporated: 30 June 2006 *Employees:* 1
Net Worth Deficit: £161,761 *Total Assets:* £89,528
Registered Office: The Old Vicarage, Awre, Newnham, Glos, GL14 1EL
Shareholders: Margery May Bull; Nicholas Bull
Officers: Margery May Bull, Secretary; Margery May Bull [1948] Director/Secretary; Nicholas Bull [1948] Director/Minerals Consultant; Thomas James Bull [1974] Director/Cider Maker

Severn Events Ltd
Incorporated: 17 November 2009
Previous: Severn Sider Ltd
Net Worth: £24,655 *Total Assets:* £45,224
Registered Office: The Old Vicarage, Awre, Newnham, Gloucester, GL14 1EL
Major Shareholder: Margery May Bull
Officers: Margery May Bull [1948] Director; Thomas James Bull [1974] Director of Severn Cider and Severn Events

Sharpham Wine Limited
Incorporated: 14 January 2019
Registered Office: Owl's Roost, Beenleigh, Harbertonford, Totnes, Devon, TQ9 7EF
Major Shareholder: Mark Richard William Sharman
Officers: Mark Richard William Sharman [1959] Director/Winemaker

Sheppy's Cider Limited
Incorporated: 13 November 2007 *Employees:* 40
Net Worth: £1,702,511 *Total Assets:* £3,427,815
Registered Office: Three Bridges, Bradford on Tone, Taunton, Somerset, TA4 1ER
Shareholders: David James Sheppy; Louisa Naomi Sheppy
Officers: Louisa Naomi Sheppy, Secretary/Manager; David James Sheppy [1966] Director/Farmer and Cider Maker; Louisa Naomi Sheppy [1962] Director/Manager

Sherborne Cider Ltd
Incorporated: 2 April 2013
Net Worth Deficit: £1,381 *Total Assets:* £5,223
Registered Office: Longburton House, Longburton, Sherborne, Dorset, DT9 5NU
Shareholders: Simon Robert Walter Baxter; Victoria Jane Baxter
Officers: Simon Robert Walter Baxter [1963] Director/Apple Grower; Victoria Jane Baxter [1966] Director/Apple Grower

Shire Meadery Ltd.
Incorporated: 15 January 2018
Registered Office: Aiec Offices, Penrhyn-Coch, Aberystwyth, Ceredigion, SY23 3EE
Major Shareholder: Benjamin David Guscott
Officers: Dr Benjamin David Guscott [1985] Director

Showerings Cider Mill Ltd
Incorporated: 14 July 2016
Net Worth Deficit: £360,544 *Total Assets:* £2,506,517
Registered Office: St Catherine's Court, Berkeley Place, Clifton, Bristol, BS8 1BQ
Parent: Brothers Drinks Co. Limited
Officers: Iain David Glen [1969] Finance Director; Jonathan Showering [1962] Director; Matthew Herbert Showering [1964] Director

The Shrewsbury Cider Company Ltd
Incorporated: 12 June 2018
Registered Office: Bank House, Main Road, Hanwood, Shrewsbury, Salop, SY5 8LY
Officers: Christopher John Oneill [1969] Director

Sibling Winery Limited
Incorporated: 19 September 2018
Registered Office: 3 Hill Top, Loxley, Warwick, CV35 9JU
Officers: Laura Marie Mitchell, Secretary; Rosanna Laura Mitchell [1990] Director; Daniel Keith Smith [1969] Director; Patrick James Smith [1969] Director

Silverpelt Ltd
Incorporated: 20 August 2018
Registered Office: 1 Mountbatten Road, Totton, Southampton, SO40 3FW
Major Shareholder: Taylor-Marie Hunt
Officers: Taylor-Marie Hunt [1997] Director/Consultant

Simoncraft Limited
Incorporated: 5 September 2018
Registered Office: 41 Woodlands Avenue, Woodley, Reading, Berks, RG5 3HN
Major Shareholder: Simon Colin Cripps
Officers: Simon Colin Cripps [1986] Director

Simply Cider Ltd
Incorporated: 5 February 2018
Registered Office: 47 Northampton Road, Market Harborough, Leics, LE16 9HB
Major Shareholder: Christopher John Baker
Officers: Christopher John Baker [1969] Director

Sky Pirate Ltd
Incorporated: 26 September 2018
Registered Office: 71-75 Shelton Street, London, WC2H 9JQ
Major Shareholder: Michael Bentley
Officers: Michael Bentley [1964] Director

SMSNaughton Ltd.
Incorporated: 5 September 2017
Net Worth: £392 *Total Assets:* £492
Registered Office: 18 Wrenthorpe Road, Bromley, Kent, BR1 5QJ
Major Shareholder: Sean Naughton
Officers: Sean Naughton [1993] Director [Irish]

Sneinton Cider Company Limited
Incorporated: 1 September 2017
Registered Office: 48 Sedgley, Sneinton, Nottingham, NG2 4HZ
Major Shareholder: James Dale Atkin
Officers: James Atkin, Secretary; James Dale Atkin, Secretary; Matt Moran, Secretary; James Dale Atkin [1989] Director/Risk Mitigation Specialist

Solway Spirits Ltd
Incorporated: 4 May 2018
Registered Office: 1 Railway Cottage, Cummertrees, Annan, Dumfries & Galloway, DG12 5QG
Major Shareholder: Andrew Emmerson
Officers: Kathryn Edith Rimmer, Secretary; Andrew Emmerson [1968] Director/Brewer and Distiller

Somerset Cider Company Limited
Incorporated: 29 October 2013
Registered Office: Higher Plot Farm, Aller Road, Langport, Somerset, TA10 0QL
Shareholder: Guy Christopher Smith
Officers: Laura Anne Evans [1962] Director/Somerset Cider Company; Guy Christopher Smith [1964] Director/Somerset Cider Company

Somerset Cider Solutions Ltd
Incorporated: 25 February 2019
Registered Office: Unit 20 Clutton Hill Farm Estate, Clutton, Bristol, BS39 5QQ
Shareholders: Richard Wilton Appleyard; Neil Carlisle MacDonald
Officers: Richard Wilton Appleyard [1985] Director; Neil Carlisle MacDonald [1967] Director

South Downs Cider Limited
Incorporated: 15 October 2018
Registered Office: Downlands, Lewes Road, Ringmer, Lewes, E Sussex, BN8 5QH
Major Shareholder: Giles Nicholas Reid
Officers: Giles Nicholas Reid [1966] Director

The Southey Brewing Company Limited
Incorporated: 15 August 2016
Net Worth Deficit: £8,345 *Total Assets:* £30,692
Registered Office: East Lodge, Bedlars Green, Great Hallingbury, Bishop's Stortford, Herts, CM22 7TL
Shareholder: Propstock Community Pubs Limited
Officers: Samuel Jonathan Barber [1986] Director/Brewer; Darren MacRae [1989] Director/Bars Manager

The Spiced Cider Company Ltd
Incorporated: 24 November 2010
Registered Office: King Arthurs Court, Maidstone Road, Charing, Ashford, Kent, TN27 0JS
Major Shareholder: Marcus Andrew Henderson
Officers: Mark Andrew Henderson [1968] Director/MD

Spinney Abbey Ltd
Incorporated: 24 August 2011
Net Worth: £8,672 *Total Assets:* £9,739
Registered Office: 35 Stretham Road, Wicken, Ely, Cambs, CB7 5XQ
Shareholders: Jonathan Steven Watkins; Jonathan Thomas Fuller
Officers: Tamsind Melissa Duffety-Fuller, Secretary; Jonathan Thomas Fuller [1978] Director/Farmer; Jonathan Steven Watkins [1979] Director/Building Maintenance

Spreyton Press Ltd.
Incorporated: 24 April 2017
Registered Office: Spreyton Barton Farm, Spreyton, Crediton, Devon, EX17 5AL
Shareholder: William Porter
Officers: William Porter [1973] Director

Spryder Ltd
Incorporated: 22 July 2016
Registered Office: 24 Hilltop Road, Berkhamsted, Herts, HP4 2HN
Shareholders: Simon Mark Spry; Graham James Ive
Officers: Graham James Ive [1991] Director/Customer Engineer; Simon Mark Spry [1991] Director/Delivery Driver

St Ives Cider Limited
Incorporated: 16 May 2012 *Employees:* 2
Net Worth Deficit: £46,488 *Total Assets:* £53,562
Registered Office: Old Mushroom Farm, Halsetown, St Ives, Cornwall, TR26 3LZ
Shareholders: Katie Berwick; David Hartley Berwick
Officers: David Hartley Berwick [1972] Director; Katie Berwick [1974] Director

Starshade Ltd
Incorporated: 1 June 2018
Registered Office: 129 Burnley Road, Padiham, Burnley, Lancs, BB12 8BA
Shareholders: Jayson Dignos; Paul Etteridge
Officers: Jayson Dignos [1998] Director [Filipino]

Still Wild Limited
Incorporated: 10 August 2018
Registered Office: Cresselly, Kilgetty, Saundersfoot, Pembrokeshire, SA68 0SP
Major Shareholder: James Alexander Hensleigh Harrison-Allen
Officers: James Alexander Hensleigh Harrison-Allen [1988] Director/Manager

Stockmoor Cider Limited
Incorporated: 24 January 2013
Net Worth Deficit: £4,838 *Total Assets:* £3,618
Registered Office: Stockmoor Court Farm, Pembridge, Leominster, Herefords, HR6 9EJ
Shareholder: James Christopher Aitchison
Officers: James Christopher Aitchison [1967] Director/Cider Maker

The Sussex South Downs Company Ltd
Incorporated: 3 April 2014
Net Worth: £6,744 *Total Assets:* £62,324
Registered Office: Windover, The Street, Selmeston, Polegate, E Sussex, BN26 6TY
Major Shareholder: Gregory Alan Meyer
Officers: Gregory Alan Meyer [1958] Director [American]; Oonagh Jane Meyer [1964] Director/Equine Consultant

Symons Cyder & Fruit Wine Co Limited
Incorporated: 6 February 2019
Registered Office: 10 Midhurst Close, Packmoor, Stoke on Trent, Staffs, ST7 4QP
Major Shareholder: Paul Albert Tranter
Officers: Paul Albert Tranter [1968] Director

TCC (Assets) Ltd
Incorporated: 27 September 2018
Registered Office: 7 John Street, London, WC1N 2ES
Major Shareholder: Abdou Razak Amadou
Officers: Abodou Razak Amadou [1986] Director; John Martin Brodie Clark [1946] Director

Tees Cider Ltd
Incorporated: 24 June 2014
Net Worth Deficit: £301 *Total Assets:* £5,261
Registered Office: Whitehall Waterfront, 2 Riverside Way, Leeds, LS1 4EH
Shareholders: Giles Duncan Ward; Julian Gaskin
Officers: Julian Anthony Gaskin [1966] Director/Solicitor; Giles Duncan Ward [1967] Director/Solicitor

Tempted Cider Company Limited
Incorporated: 7 July 2015
Net Worth: £496 *Total Assets:* £65,519
Registered Office: 155-157 Donegall Pass, Belfast, BT7 1DT
Shareholder: Steven Clark Pattison
Officers: Steven Clark Pattison [1979] Director; Richard Henderson Ryan [1977] Director/Designer; David James Uprichard [1960] Director; Janet Estelle Barnett Uprichard [1957] Director

Ten Tors Brewery Ltd
Incorporated: 5 February 2018
Registered Office: 71-75 Shelton Street, Covent Garden, London, WC2H 9JQ
Major Shareholder: Daryl Hall
Officers: Daryl Hall [1984] Director/HGV Driver

Thatchers Cider Company Limited
Incorporated: 13 June 1955 *Employees:* 166
Net Worth: £16,292,184 *Total Assets:* £52,640,336
Registered Office: Myrtle Farm, Station Road, Sandford, Winscombe, Avon, BS25 5RA
Officers: Robert Graham Davis [1947] Director; Neil Day [1973] Director/Engineer; Lord Digby Jones [1955] Director; Graham Andrew Keating [1964] Director; Christopher Milton [1963] Sales Director; Robert Charles Sandall [1968] Director; Martin Thatcher [1968] Director/Cider Manufacturer; Rupert Geoffrey Ryland Thompson [1958] Director

Thistly Cross Cider Co Limited
Incorporated: 29 December 2010 *Employees:* 21
Net Worth: £1,182,958 *Total Assets:* £1,541,614
Registered Office: c/o Ledingham Chalmers LLP, 3rd Floor, 68-70 George Street, Edinburgh, EH2 2LR
Shareholders: Dunsmore Family Holdings Limited; Peter Neilson Stuart
Officers: John Michael Dunsmore [1959] Director; Lynne Dunsmore [1961] Director; Peter Neilson Stuart [1975] Director/Cidermaker

Thompstone Industries Ltd.
Incorporated: 29 June 2017
Net Worth: £200 *Total Assets:* £200
Registered Office: The Cider Barn, 1 Caddaford Court, Buckfastleigh, Newton Abbot, Devon, TQ11 0JT
Major Shareholder: Andrew Thompstone
Officers: Andrew Thompstone [1969] Director/Cider Maker and Rope Worker

Tiddly Pommes Ltd
Incorporated: 17 October 2016
Net Worth: £33,965 *Total Assets:* £80,733
Registered Office: 6 London Place, Oxford, OX4 1BD
Major Shareholder: Rupert Ivor James Griffin
Officers: Hannah Clare Fenton [1983] Director/Marketing and Sales; Rupert Ivor James Griffin [1971] Director/Fruit Juice Manufacturer; Antony Richard David Melville [1952] Director/Publisher (Retired)

Tinston Wines & Ciders Limited
Incorporated: 2 October 2017
Registered Office: 24 Crayford Road, Brighton, BN2 4DQ
Major Shareholder: Liam Tinston
Officers: Liam Tinston [1984] Director/Winemaker

Tip Tap & Top Ltd
Incorporated: 26 February 2016
Net Worth Deficit: £25,189 *Total Assets:* £5,124
Registered Office: 9 Broadbeck, Waddingham, Gainsborough, Lincs, DN21 4TH
Shareholders: Ron Edgar; Margaret Edgar
Officers: Margaret Edgar [1951] Director/Retired; Matthew Leonard Edgar [1984] Director; Ronald Edgar [1949] Director/Sales Person

Toby's Cider Limited
Incorporated: 26 March 2013
Net Worth Deficit: £32,604 *Total Assets:* £4,612
Registered Office: 76-78 Church Street, Portadown, Co Armagh, BT62 3EU
Shareholders: Craig John Shipman; Karen Elizabeth Shipman
Officers: Craig John Shipman [1976] Director; Karen Elizabeth Shipman [1973] Director

Torre Cider Co Ltd
Incorporated: 20 July 2015
Net Worth: £11,090   *Total Assets:* £379,349
Registered Office: Torre Cider Farm, Torre, Washford, Watchet, Somerset, TA23 0LA
Shareholders: Gemma May Combe; Neil James Freeman
Officers: Gemma May Combe, Secretary; Gemma May Combe [1982] Director; Neil James Freeman [1978] Director

Tremayne Food and Drink Limited
Incorporated: 10 January 2019
Registered Office: The Old Nuclear Bunker, Pednavounder, Coverack, Cornwall, TR12 6SE
Shareholders: Mark Stephen Nattrass; Leonora Helen Nattrass
Officers: Dr Mark Stephen Nattrass [1966] Director

Trinity Orchards Limited
Incorporated: 25 June 2014
Previous: Trinity Drinks Limited
Registered Office: 1 Barcham Cottages, Barcham Road, Barcham, Soham, Cambs, CB7 5TU
Major Shareholder: David Reynold Henry
Officers: David Reynold Henry [1960] Director/Food & Drink

Tripper Cider Ltd
Incorporated: 6 August 2018
Registered Office: 61B Ongar Road, London, SW6 1SH
Major Shareholder: Grania Alexandra Louise Howard
Officers: Grania Alexandra Louise Howard [1988] Director

Turbo Cider Limited
Incorporated: 7 December 2017
Registered Office: 17 Bobbin Close, Golcar, Huddersfield, W Yorks, HD7 4DQ
Major Shareholder: David Hinchliffe
Officers: David Hinchliffe [1970] Director

Tutts Clump Cider Ltd
Incorporated: 18 November 2008
Net Worth: £223,909   *Total Assets:* £314,501
Registered Office: Travellers Rest Farm, Hungerford Lane, Bradfield, Reading, Berks, RG7 6JH
Major Shareholder: Timothy Gilbert Wale
Officers: Catherine Wale, Secretary; Lucy Catherine Wale [1991] Director; Timothy Gilbert Wale [1957] Director/Motor Engineer

Twin Barrel Brewery Limited
Incorporated: 24 December 2018
Registered Office: 45 Whitecross Avenue, Bristol, BS14 9JF
Shareholders: Brett John Williams; ABW Global Limited
Officers: Brett John Williams [1993] Director/Co-Founder

Ty Gwyn Cider Limited
Incorporated: 29 May 2014
Net Worth: £16,463   *Total Assets:* £209,667
Registered Office: Penylan Farm, Pontrilas, Herefords, HR2 0DL
Major Shareholder: Alexander Harry Culpin
Officers: Alexander Harry Culpin [1969] Director/Cider Maker

Umbrella Brewing Limited
Incorporated: 28 July 2015   *Employees:* 4
Net Worth Deficit: £70,034   *Total Assets:* £115,512
Registered Office: 626a Holloway Road, London, N19 3PA
Shareholders: Alastair Charles Tatton; Stephen Robert Thompson; Andrew James Kerr; Matthew Graham Armitage
Officers: Matthew Graham Armitage [1984] Director; Andrew James Kerr [1979] Director; Alastair Charles Tatton [1982] Director; Stephen Robert Thompson [1987] Director

Vachery Farm Cider Limited
Incorporated: 22 September 2016
Net Worth Deficit: £942   *Total Assets:* £8,382
Registered Office: Vachery Farm Estate Office, Horsham Road, Cranleigh, Surrey, GU6 8EJ
Shareholders: Nicolas Victor Cook; Peter George O'Connor
Officers: Eimear Moulds Cook [1968] Director; Peter George O'Connor [1981] Director

The Viking Winery Ltd
Incorporated: 15 June 2016
Registered Office: 43 Rockliffe Road, Bath, BA2 6QW
Officers: Craig Aaron Whittock [1988] Director

Virtual Orchard Limited
Incorporated: 7 August 2012
Net Worth Deficit: £59,888   *Total Assets:* £20,252
Registered Office: 16 High Street, Potterspury, Towcester, Northants, NN12 7PQ
Major Shareholder: Laurence Nigel Conisbee
Officers: Laurence Nigel Conisbee [1968] Director

W & W Drinks Ltd
Incorporated: 9 January 2019
Registered Office: Unit 2 Broadview Farm, The Ridge, Cold Ash, Thatcham, Berks, RG18 9HX
Shareholders: Gary Christopher Wickens; Richard Anthony Wyatt
Officers: Gary Christopher Wickens [1977] Director; Richard Anthony Wyatt [1977] Director

Wadys Cider Limited
Incorporated: 2 May 2017
Net Worth Deficit: £8,289   *Total Assets:* £7,365
Registered Office: 14 Hector Road, Catcott, Bridgwater, Somerset, TA7 9HL
Major Shareholder: Christopher Wady
Officers: Christopher Wady [1990] Director

Hiram Walker (UK) Limited
Incorporated: 20 September 1932
Registered Office: Chivas House, 72 Chancellors Road, London, W6 9RS
Parent: Allied Domecq Spirits & Wine Limited
Officers: Stuart MacNab [1964] Director/Accountant; Vincent Turpin [1978] Director/Chief Financial Officer [French]

Wasted Apple Co Ltd
Incorporated: 14 November 2014
Net Worth Deficit: £3,346   *Total Assets:* £5,265
Registered Office: Southwinds, Porthpean Beach Road, St Austell, Cornwall, PL26 6AU
Officers: Mark Andrew Rudge [1969] Director/Local Government

Wasted Opportunity Limited
Incorporated: 26 March 2018
Registered Office: 27 Old Gloucester Street, London, WC1N 3AX
Major Shareholder: Ross Evans
Officers: Ross Evans [1981] Director

Wessex Cider Limited
Incorporated: 14 October 2009   *Employees:* 1
Net Worth Deficit: £27,398   *Total Assets:* £43,712
Registered Office: The Rafters, Manor Farm, Bishopstone, Salisbury, Wilts, SP5 4AS
Shareholders: Nigel Anthony Gouterais Cuff; Joanna Cuff
Officers: Joanna Cuff [1968] Director; Nigel Anthony Gouterais Cuff [1965] Director

Wessex Drinks Company Limited
Incorporated: 14 October 2009
Registered Office: The Rafters, Manor Farm, Bishopstone, Salisbury, Wilts, SP5 4AS
Shareholders: Nigel Anthony Gouterais Cuff; Joanna Cuff
Officers: Joanna Cuff [1968] Director; Nigel Anthony Gouterais Cuff [1965] Director/Photographer

The Wessex Wild Plum Company Limited
Incorporated: 8 March 2011
Net Worth Deficit: £149,809 *Total Assets:* £156,598
Registered Office: Old Stable House, Lower Chilland Lane, Martyr Worthy, Winchester, Hants, SO21 1EB
Officers: James William Parry [1965] Director/Consultant

Westmoor Botanicals Limited
Incorporated: 22 November 2018
Registered Office: 132 Ravenstone Drive, Greetland, Halifax, W Yorks, HX4 8DY
Shareholder: Philip George Scoley
Officers: Helen Rose-Marie Scoley [1966] Director/Teacher; Philip George Scoley [1962] Director/Management Consultant

H.Weston & Sons Limited
Incorporated: 11 October 1960 *Employees:* 236
Net Worth: £26,748,896 *Total Assets:* £42,667,464
Registered Office: The Bounds, Much Marcle, Ledbury, Herefords, HR8 2NQ
Shareholders: Helen Maureen Thomas; Timothy John Hubert Weston; Henry Norman Weston
Officers: Patrick Matthew Smith, Secretary; Geoffrey Nigel Bradman [1958] Commercial Director; David Griffiths [1963] Operations Director; Richard John Price [1956] Director/Accountant; Helen Maureen Thomas [1953] Managing Director/Company Secretary; Henry Norman Weston [1954] Director; Timothy John Hubert Weston [1958] Director

Whin Hill (Norfolk) Cider Ltd
Incorporated: 17 January 2012 *Employees:* 2
Net Worth: £42,230 *Total Assets:* £136,568
Registered Office: Summerhill House, Sculthorpe Road, Fakenham, Norfolk, NR21 9HA
Shareholders: Lisa Jane Jarvis; Mark William Jarvis
Officers: Lisa Jane Jarvis, Secretary; Lisa Jane Jarvis [1971] Director; Mark William Jarvis [1969] Director/Cider Producer

Whin Hill Cider Limited
Incorporated: 3 February 1998
Net Worth: £393,885 *Total Assets:* £402,579
Registered Office: Fountain House, Bases Lane, Wells-Next-The-Sea, Norfolk, NR23 1BT
Shareholders: James William Fergusson; Peter Phillip Lynn
Officers: James Fergusson, Secretary/Cider Maker; James Fergusson [1951] Director/Cider Maker; Peter Phillip Lynn [1949] Director/Cider Maker

White Heron Brands Limited
Incorporated: 26 May 2016 *Employees:* 3
Net Worth Deficit: £125,792 *Total Assets:* £258,350
Registered Office: Next End Farm, Lyonshall, Kington, Herefords, HR5 3JA
Major Shareholder: Joanna Phyllis Hilditch
Officers: Peter John Andrew [1965] Director; Joanna Phyllis Hilditch [1964] Director/Farmer

White Rose Cider Limited
Incorporated: 19 September 2016
Net Worth Deficit: £9,326 *Total Assets:* £1,026
Registered Office: Sigglesthorne Grange, Great Hatfield Road, Sigglesthorne, Hull, HU11 5QJ
Officers: David Close [1953] Joint Director; Simon Roberts [1970] Joint Director; Alan Smith [1951] Joint Director

Wibblers Brewery (Farms) Limited
Incorporated: 13 May 2010
Net Worth: £23,970 *Total Assets:* £187,463
Registered Office: Wibblers Brewery, Goldsands Road, Southminster, Essex, CM0 7JW
Shareholders: Philip John Wilcox; Abigayle Margaret Wilcox; Jeremy John Wilcox
Officers: Abigayle Wilcox [1980] Director; Jeremy John Wilcox [1942] Director/Retired; Philip John Wilcox [1973] Director

Wide Eyes Enterprises Limited
Incorporated: 3 April 2017
Registered Office: Kincraigie, Over Ross Street, Ross on Wye, Herefords, HR9 7AU
Major Shareholder: Joseph Lewis Bartholemew Scott
Officers: Joseph Lewis Bartholemew Scott [1987] Director/Salesman

Wild Cider Limited
Incorporated: 5 November 2015
Registered Office: Cockerels Corner, Pitt Court, North Nibley, Dursley, Glos, GL11 6EB
Officers: John Barnes [1971] Director/Cider Production

Wild Life Botanicals Ltd
Incorporated: 28 February 2019
Registered Office: 20-22 Wenlock Road, London, N1 7GU
Major Shareholder: Jonathan Paul Steadman Archer
Officers: Jonathan Paul Steadman Archer [1966] Director

Wimborne Cider Company Limited
Incorporated: 6 June 2012
Registered Office: Merry Hill Cottage, Long Lane, Wimborne, Dorset, BH21 7AQ
Shareholders: Louise Elizabeth Cox; David Alastair Douglas Sandbach
Officers: Louise Elizabeth Cox, Secretary; David Alastair Douglas Sandbach [1980] Dircctor/HR Consultant

Wise Owl Cider Ltd
Incorporated: 10 July 2012
Net Worth Deficit: £56,011 *Total Assets:* £58,973
Registered Office: Vine Hall Farm, Bethersden, Ashford, Kent, TN26 3JY
Major Shareholder: Richard John Wise
Officers: Paula Wise, Secretary; Paula Wise [1964] Director/Cider Maker; Richard John Wise [1969] Director/Cider Maker

Woodstar Limited
Incorporated: 9 March 2017
Registered Office: 54 Hillbury Avenue, Harrow, Middlesex, HA3 8EW
Major Shareholder: Andrew Stanley Baker
Officers: Andrew Stanley Baker [1959] Director

Worleys Cider Limited
Incorporated: 24 October 2009
Net Worth: £39,158 *Total Assets:* £74,212
Registered Office: 55 Dean, Shepton Mallet, Somerset, BA4 4SA
Shareholders: Helen Louise Burge; Neil John Worley
Officers: Helen Louise Burge, Secretary; Helen Louise Burge [1968] Director; Neil John Worley [1966] Director

Wye Valley Meadery Ltd
Incorporated: 14 September 2017
Registered Office: 19 River View, School Hill, Chepstow, Monmouthshire, NP16 5AX
Shareholders: Christopher John Newell; Matthew David Newell
Officers: Christopher John Newell [1990] Director/Co-Founder; Matthew David Newell [1989] Director/Co-Founder

Zymurgorium Ltd
Incorporated: 13 September 2016 *Employees:* 3
Net Worth: £447,149 *Total Assets:* £765,763
Registered Office: Unit B6, Fairhills Road, Irlam, Manchester, M44 6BA
Major Shareholder: Aaron Ross Darke
Officers: Aaron Ross Darke [1991] Distiller/Brewer Managing Director; Callum Thomas Darke [1989] Director/Operations/Accounts Manager

Index of Directorships

Abbiss, Karen Sarah
Abbiss Drinks Co Ltd

Abbiss, Simon Timothy
Abbiss Drinks Co Ltd

Abbott, Joe Marley
Iford Cider Limited

Abel, Harold
Old Tree Brewery Ltd

Aberdeen, Martin John
House Brewery Limited

Adcock, Gary George
Dorset Orchards Limited

Ademola, Adekunle Akanji
Fruito Soft Drinks Limited

Aitchison, James Christopher
Stockmoor Cider Limited

Aje, Benson
BF Wines UK Ltd

Albini, Paul Anthony
The Lambswick Drinks Co Ltd

Allen, Alastair
The Appletreewick Cider Co Ltd

Alsabah, Eman Nasser Sabah Alnasser
Nada General Trading Ltd

Amadou, Abodou Razak
TCC (Assets) Ltd

Anagnostopoulos, George
The Husthwaite Orchard Village Ltd

Andrew, Peter John
White Heron Brands Limited

Appleyard, Richard Wilton
Somerset Cider Solutions Ltd

Archer, Jonathan Paul Steadman
Wild Life Botanicals Ltd

Armitage, Matthew Graham
Umbrella Brewing Limited

Armstrong, Peter Michael
Thomas Hardy Kendal Limited

Arthur, Daniel
Bhat Ltd.

Ash, Jason James Sproule
The Orchard Pig Ltd

Atkin, James Dale
Sneinton Cider Co Ltd

Atkin, Jonathan
Noahs Estate Ltd

Atkinson, Peter David
The Rutland Cider Co Ltd

Audrey, Beauce Lyvio
Bobo Roots Wine Ltd

Aylward, Kieran
London Cider Co Ltd
Olde Mill Ltd

Bailey, David
The Green Shed Cider Co Ltd

Bailey, Margaret
Hartpury Heritage Trust

Baker, Andrew Stanley
Woodstar Limited

Baker, Christopher John
Simply Cider Ltd

Ball, Keith Michael
Lyme Bay Cider Co Ltd
Lyme Bay Winery Limited

Banks, Samuel N K
AB Vaults Group Limited

Barber, Samuel Jonathan
The Southey Brewing Co Ltd

Barnes, John
Wild Cider Limited

Barnes, Richard Julian
Biddenden Vineyards Limited

Barnes, Sally
Biddenden Vineyards Limited

Baxter, Simon Robert Walter
Sherborne Cider Ltd

Baxter, Victoria Jane
Sherborne Cider Ltd

Beasley, Andrew Robert
Lyme Bay Cider Co Ltd
Lyme Bay Winery Limited

Beattie, Robert
The Malmesbury Cider Co Ltd

Bell, Robert
Broadland Wineries Limited

Bellena, Clarita
Farcial Ltd

Benson, Alexia Louise
Bensons Fruit Juice Limited

Benson, Jeremy
Bensons Fruit Juice Limited
Dunkertons Cider Co Ltd

Bentley, Michael
Sky Pirate Ltd

Bergius, Brock Ninian Sanderson
Gospel Green Cyder Co Ltd

Berwick, David Hartley
St Ives Cider Limited

Berwick, Katie
St Ives Cider Limited

Billing, Martyn John
Ascension Cider Co. Limited

Billing, Matthew David Anthony
Ascension Cider Co. Limited

Birchall, Elaine
Merrydown PLC

Blandford-Newson, Christopher John
Distell International Holdings Ltd

Bonan, Mary Elaine
Arkustemple Ltd

Boscawen, Evelyn George William
Marourde Limited

Bowen, Elsie
Appledunc Limited

Boyd, Martin James
The New Union Brewing Co Ltd

Bradbury, John Andrew
Halewood International Limited

Bradley, Jeffrey Charles Richard
Hidden Orchard Ltd

Bradman, Geoffrey Nigel
H.Weston & Sons Limited

Braham, Malcolm Ernest
The Halfpenny Green Cider Co Ltd

Brunt, Nina Maria Emily
Broadoak Cider Co Ltd

Brunt, Steven Lee
Broadoak Cider Co Ltd

Bryan, Neville Patrick
The Garden Cider Co Ltd

Buchan, James Alexander Stephen
3CS Cider Limited

Buckland, Neale Antony
Chase Cider Limited

Buckley, William Howard
Grumpy Frog Ltd

Budd, Anthony James
Kingscote Winery Ltd

Bugg, David Michael
Old Town Brewery Ltd.

Bull, Margery May
Severn Events Ltd
Severn Cider Ltd

Bull, Nicholas
Severn Cider Ltd

Bull, Thomas James
Severn Cider Ltd
Severn Events Ltd

Bulmer, Theodore Tobias
King Offa Ltd

Bunyan, Katherine
Puxted Cider Limited

Bunyan, Martin John
Puxted Cider Limited

Burge, Helen Louise
Worleys Cider Limited

Burgis, Gillian
Broxbourne Brewery Ltd.

Burnett, Duncan Walker
Salcombe Cider Co Ltd

Butler, Emily Alice
The Big Bear Cider Mill Ltd

Butterfield, William
Green Valley Cyder Limited
Sandford Orchards Limited

Buxton, Ann
Medlar Management Limited

Buxton, Edward John
Medlar Management Limited

Byrom, Gary
Bhat Ltd.

Calver, Jonathan Charles
Branded Drinks Ltd

Caney, John Edward
Caneys Cider Ltd

Caney, Victoria Anne
Caneys Cider Ltd

Carter, Andrew James
Jars Cider Ltd

Cartwright-Hignett, Marianne Lucy
Iford Cider Limited

Cartwright-Hignett, William Fairfax
Iford Cider Limited

Casling, Lyn Howell
Gwynt y Ddraig Cider Ltd

Caton, Matthew James
Last Sign Brewing Co Ltd

Chapillon, Neil
Ham Hill Cider Limited

Chapman, Alison Boyd
Harry's Cider Co Ltd

Chapman, Holly Bridget
Hartpury Heritage Trust
Hartpury Process Limited

Chapman, James Roger
Hartpury Heritage Trust
Hartpury Process Limited

Chapman, Timothy James
Giggler Ltd

Cheetham, Dominic Knight
The Chiltern Cider Co Ltd

Chissell Topp, Barry John
New Forest Cider Limited

Churchward, Martin John
The Lambswick Drinks Co Ltd

Clark, John Martin Brodie
TCC (Assets) Ltd

Clark, Matthew Nicolas
Embev Ltd

Clay, Imogen Sarah
Medlar Management Limited

Close, David
White Rose Cider Limited

Cole, Marc Andrew Richard
Colemans Cider Co Ltd

Coles, Christopher John, Dr
Marsh Barton Farm Cyder Ltd

Coles, Elzbieta Eugenia
Marsh Barton Farm Cyder Ltd

Coles, Gerard Peter
Honey & Daughter Limited

Collighan, Giles Thomas
The Portsmouth Distillery Co Ltd

Combe, Gemma May
Torre Cider Co Ltd

Comer, Katherine Ruth
East Coast Cider Co Ltd

Comer, Ruth
Harleston Cider Co Ltd

Conisbee, Laurence Nigel
Virtual Orchard Limited

Conte, Marko
Conte International Limited

Cook, Eimear Moulds
Vachery Farm Cider Limited

Cook, Hiranthi Generaldine
Cooks Cider Ltd

Cook, Irma
Organic Country Drinks Ltd

Cook, Jeremy Mark
Missing Link Brewing Ltd

Cook, Matthew
Cooks Cider Ltd

Cook, Sebastian
Cooks Cider Ltd

Cook, William Roy
Organic Country Drinks Ltd

Cooper, Samuel Charles Orlando
Black Dog Meadery Ltd

Corke, Adrian
Peak Ciders Limited

Coulson, John Paul
Polgoon Vineyard Ltd

Courage, Christopher John
Brothers Drinks Co. Limited

Crawford, Kelly Elizabeth
Armagh Cider Co Ltd

Cripps, Simon Colin
Simoncraft Limited

Cuff, Joanna
Wessex Cider Limited
Wessex Drinks Co Ltd

Cuff, Nigel Anthony Gouterais
Wessex Cider Limited
Wessex Drinks Co Ltd

Culpin, Alexander Harry
Ty Gwyn Cider Limited

Culpin, Benedict Alan
Apple County Cider Co Limited

Culpin, Stephanie Adele Acton
Apple County Cider Co Limited

Dalrymple BT, Hew Richard Hamilton
Broadland Wineries Limited

Dampney, Jonathan Nicholas
Dampney's Remarkable Drinks Ltd.

Dampney, Richard John
Dampney's Remarkable Drinks Ltd.

Daniell, Thomas Charles Averell
Old Tree Brewery Ltd

Darke, Aaron Ross
Zymurgorium Ltd

Darke, Callum Thomas
Zymurgorium Ltd

Darrall, Sabine Claire
Lyne Down Organics Limited

Daughtrey, Barbara Ann
A Little Luxury Distillery Ltd

Daughtrey, Laura Elizabeth
A Little Luxury Distillery Ltd

David, Jhonafe
Diamations Ltd

Davis, Nicholas Edward James
The Lambswick Drinks Co Ltd

Davis, Robert Graham
Thatchers Cider Co Ltd

Davis, William Anthony
The Rutland Cider Co Ltd

Davison, Angus James
Haygrove Evolution Limited

Dawe, James
Colourful Outbursts Limited

Day, Neil
Thatchers Cider Co Ltd

Day, Simon Richard
Haygrove Evolution Limited

De Vos, Benjamin
Bitter & Sweet UK Ltd

Dickie, Alan Martin
Hawkes Cider Limited

Dickson, Fiona Jayne
Legiste Limited

Dignos, Jayson
Starshade Ltd

Dinnage, Elizabeth Claire
Chucklehead Cider Ltd

Dinnage, Michael John
Chucklehead Cider Ltd

Dodd, Simon Ray
Cornish Orchards Ltd

Douglas, Ian Alan
H & A Prestige Bottling Ltd

Douglas-Hamilton, James David Cameron
The Cotswold Cider Co Ltd

Drury, Pauline
Hartpury Heritage Trust

Dunkerton, Julian Marc
Dunkertons Cider Co Ltd

Dunn, Thomas James William
Beard and Sabre Ltd.

Dunsmore, John Michael
Thistly Cross Cider Co Limited

Dunsmore, Lynne
Thistly Cross Cider Co Limited

Dyer, George Peter
The Gentleman's Cider Ltd.

Earle, James Matthew
The Cheltenham Cider Co Ltd

Eaton, Peter Gary
H & A Prestige Bottling Ltd
Halewood International Limited

Edgar, Margaret
Marron (Lincoln) Ltd
Tip Tap & Top Ltd

Edgar, Matthew Leonard
Cool Brew Dept Ltd
Tip Tap & Top Ltd

Edgar, Ronald
Marron (Lincoln) Ltd
Tip Tap & Top Ltd

Edioma, Alan
Calmcorn Ltd

Edmonds, Mark
Ham Hill Cider Limited

Ellis, Gareth
Lancashire Cider Limited

Ellis, James Douglas
Aston Manor Limited

Emeny, Simon
Cornish Orchards Ltd

Emmerson, Andrew
Solway Spirits Ltd

Evans, Ian
Gwynt y Ddraig Cider Ltd

Evans, John Griffiths
Hartpury Heritage Trust

Evans, Laura Anne
Somerset Cider Co Ltd

Evans, Ross
Wasted Opportunity Limited

Fawcett, Lucifer
Luminati Wine Limited

Fenton, Hannah Clare
Tiddly Pommes Ltd

Fenton, Sophia Emma
Cornish Mead Co.Limited

Fergusson, James
Whin Hill Cider Limited

Fernandes, Clive
Himachal Ltd

Ferrari, Angelo
Laycock Cider Ltd

Filby, Benjamin James
The Garden Cider Co Ltd

Filby, William Jack
The Garden Cider Co Ltd

Fitch, Jonathan Matthew
Polecat Cider Limited

Fleming, Sean Woelfell
Little Wolf Brewing Limited

Fletcher, Simon Rayland Hewitt
Bevisol Limited

Ford, Peter James
Orchard Origins C.I.C.

Forde, David Michael
H P Bulmer Limited

Fordham, Christopher Michael Peter
Dean Press Cider Ltd.

Foster, George
Revenant Cider Limited

France, Denis
Handmade Cider Co Ltd

Fred, Collin
Highworth Cider and Perry Ltd

Freeman, Neil James
Torre Cider Co Ltd

Fry, Harry Stewart
Harry's Cider Co Ltd

Fuller, Jonathan Thomas
Spinney Abbey Ltd

Fuller, Richard Hamilton Fleetwood
Cornish Orchards Ltd

Galbraith, James Joseph
L'Atypique Ltd

Galloway, Jasper Rory Barrington
3CS Cider Limited

Gandhi, Ritam
Cider Mill Limited

Garrod, Paul John
Bockleton Court Limited

Gaskin, Julian Anthony
Tees Cider Ltd

Gibson, Craig
Ginsecco Ltd

Gilbert, Helen Isabelle
Islay Wines Ltd

Gillies, Judith
Cairn O'Mohr Ltd.

Gillies, Ronald Andrew
Cairn O'Mohr Ltd.

Glancey, Stephen
Gaymer Cider Co Ltd
Magners GB Limited

Glen, Iain David
Brothers Drinks Co. Limited
Showerings Cider Mill Ltd

Gloeckner, Phillipa Nickerson
Damsons in Distress Limited

Glyn, Richard Rufus Francis
Brewers Folly Brewery Ltd.

Goff, Timothy Robert
Halewood International Limited

Goldsmith, Michelle
The Radnage Cider Co Ltd

Graeber, Grant Kelly
The Mad Yank Brewery Ltd

Graeber, Larissa Michelle
The Mad Yank Brewery Ltd

Grainger, Richard Stuart
The Long Ashton Cider Co Ltd

Grant, Gregor James
Essex Cider Co Ltd

Greatorex, Sam, Dr
Jars Cider Ltd

Green, Alexander Barnaby
Heron Valley Cider Limited

Green, Laurence John
Orchard Origins C.I.C.

Green, Natasha
Heron Valley Cider Limited

Griffin, Rupert Ivor James
Tiddly Pommes Ltd

Griffiths, David
H.Weston & Sons Limited

Gronow, Andrew
Gwynt y Ddraig Cider Ltd

Gudonis, Paul
Revenant Cider Limited

Guscott, Benjamin David, Dr
Shire Meadery Ltd.

Gwatkin, Denis Edward Charles
Gwatkin Cider Co. Limited

Gwatkin, Eric William John
Gwatkin Cider Co. Limited

Habich-Crayton, Aleksandra Maria
Dunwrights Cider Co Ltd

Hafstad, Einar Finn
Medland Manor Vineyard Ltd.

Hainsworth, Stewart Andrew
H & A Prestige Bottling Ltd
Halewood International Limited

Halewood, Judith Margaret
H & A Prestige Bottling Ltd
Halewood International Limited

Hall, Daryl
Ten Tors Brewery Ltd

Halsted, David Michael
Pembrokeshire Cider Limited

Hancocks, Robert James
Celtic Marches Beverages Ltd
Marches Bottling and Packaging Ltd

Harding, Fionagh Mason
North Coast Cider Co Ltd

Harding, Philip Josiah
Revenant Cider Limited

Harding, Richard William
North Coast Cider Co Ltd

Hardingham, Barbara Eileen
Ludlow Vineyard Limited

Hardingham, Michael John
Ludlow Vineyard Limited

Harris, Dean Patrick
Brewers Folly Brewery Ltd.

Harrison, Ivor John Anthony
Cranes Drink Ltd

Harrison-Allen, James Alexander Hensleigh
Still Wild Limited

Hart, Bryan Seymour
The Chiltern Cider Co Ltd

Hart, Christopher Philip
The Not Real Wine Co Ltd

Hartle, Joesph
The Purbeck Cider Co Ltd

Hartnoll, Peter Walden
Ostlers Cider Mill Limited

Hawkins, Martin John
Hawkins Drinks Limited

Hawrylak, Alejandro Marzana
Alejandro's Wines Limited

Hayden, Patrick
Saint Patricks Ltd

Heads, Kevin
Isle of Islay Cider Co Ltd

Healey, David John
Cornish Scrumpy Co Ltd
Cornish Scrumpy Holdings Ltd

Healey, Jonathon
Cornish Scrumpy Co Ltd
Cornish Scrumpy Holdings Ltd

Healey, Kay Victoria
Cornish Scrumpy Co Ltd
Cornish Scrumpy Holdings Ltd

Healey, Sam
Cornish Scrumpy Co Ltd
Cornish Scrumpy Holdings Ltd

Hecks, Christopher Edgar
The Glastonbury Drinks Co Ltd

Hecks, Sandra Pamela
The Glastonbury Drinks Co Ltd

Heffernan, Maureen
The Garden Cider Co Ltd

Heffernan, Riona
Gaymer Cider Co Ltd

Heley, Joseph Peter
Secret Orchard Cider Ltd

Henderson, Christopher Ian
Brewbarb Ltd
Broobarb Ltd

Henderson, Mark Andrew
Kent Cider Co Ltd
The Spiced Cider Co Ltd

Henney, Mike
Henney's Cider Co Ltd

Henry, David Reynold
Trinity Orchards Limited

Higginson, George Pires
Samba Cidra Ltd

Hilditch, Joanna Phyllis
White Heron Brands Limited

Hinchliffe, David
Pennine Cider Limited
Turbo Cider Limited

Hines, Timothy Richard
Halewood International Limited

Hogan, Allen Patrick
Hogan's Cider Limited

Holmes, Donald Alexander
Isle of Mull Winery Ltd

Honey, Robert George
Honey & Daughter Limited

Horan, Nicholas William
Apple Hoarders Limited

House, Frances Bryony
The Cotswold Fruit Co Ltd.

Howard, Grania Alexandra Louise
Tripper Cider Ltd

Howarth, Jonathan Hamilton
Lost Boys Brewery Ltd

Hubert, Timothy
The Long Ashton Cider Co Ltd

Hudson, Richard Selby
Broadlands Cider Farm Limited

Hughes, Kathryn Ella
The Big Bear Cider Mill Ltd

Hughes, William Michael
The Big Bear Cider Mill Ltd

Hunt, John Simon
Broughton Ales Limited

Hunt, Richard George
Hunt's Cider Limited

Hunt, Taylor-Marie
Silverpelt Ltd

Hurd, Kelvin
Laughing Ass Brewery Ltd

Hurdwell, Kevin
The Fermentorium Ltd

Hurrell, Brian Peter Robert
Orchard Origins C.I.C.

Hurst, Anne-Marie
The Flower Miners Limited

Husband, Andrew James
AA & D Limited
Caledonia Cider Limited

Imlach, Robert Francis
Liberty Orchards Limited

Irvine, David Andrew
Brute Brewing Co Ltd

Isaac, Kevin Paul, Dr
Barton Cider Co Ltd

Ive, Graham James
Spryder Ltd

Jackson, Steven
Colemans Cider Co Ltd

Jacobs, Yves
Aston Manor Limited

Jagels, Kay Dawn
Duxford Scrumpy Co Ltd

James, Annette Christine
Hunt's Cider Limited

Jarvis, Lisa Jane
Whin Hill (Norfolk) Cider Ltd

Jarvis, Mark William
Whin Hill (Norfolk) Cider Ltd

Jassal, Harmesh Lal
Colemans Cider Co Ltd

Jelfs, Nigel Desmond
Noddy's Cider Ltd

Jenner, Thomas Edward
Bumble Mead Ltd

Jewkes, Lawrence
Revenant Cider Limited

Johncox, Gordon Paul Hazell
Aston Manor Limited

Johnson, Albert James
Ross-on-Wye Cider & Perry Co Ltd

Johnson, Charlotte Frances
Meon Valley Cider Ltd

Johnson, Christopher Scott
Dee Ciders Limited

Johnson, Michael James
Ross-on-Wye Cider & Perry Co Ltd

Johnson, Nigel Douglas Hamilton
Meon Valley Cider Ltd

Johnson, Rhys
Crosby Beverages Ltd

Johnson, Richard Michael
Dee Ciders Limited

Johnson, Timothy Robert
Frampton Farm Limited

Jolmes, Nikolas
Lisnisky Cider Co Ltd

Jones, Derek Ian
DJ Wines Limited

Jones, Digby, Lord
Thatchers Cider Co Ltd

Jones, Eve Beryl
Old Tree Brewery Ltd

Jones, Richard Neil
DJ Wines Limited

Keating, Graham Andrew
Thatchers Cider Co Ltd

Keegan, Steve James
Holler Brewery Limited

Kemp, Martin
The London Beer Co Ltd

Kerr, Andrew James
Umbrella Brewing Limited

Kinghan, Anneka
Crai Cider Co Ltd

Kinghan, Stephen
Crai Cider Co Ltd

Kirwin, Daniel Mark
H & A Prestige Bottling Ltd

Kitt, Joshua James
Lost Boys Brewery Ltd

Lambert, James Lawrence
Lyme Bay Cider Co Ltd
Lyme Bay Winery Limited

Lancaster, David Albert
Thomas Paine Brewery Limited

Lansley, Jonathon Mark
Broadland Wineries Limited

Layton, Claire
The Orgasmic Cider Co. Ltd

Layton, Stephen Denis
The Orgasmic Cider Co. Ltd

Layton, William Andrew
The Orgasmic Cider Co. Ltd

Leather, Angus Peter Michael
Appledunc Limited

Leather, Emily Laura Jane
Appledunc Limited

Lee, Anna Lena
Ashgrove Farm Produce Ltd

Lee, Gareth Derek
The Kinross Brewery Limited

Leiworthy, Matthew Thomas
Cornish Mead Co.Limited

Leiworthy, Sidney Thomas
Cornish Mead Co.Limited

Lemmey, Alison Jean
Liberty Orchards Limited

Lemmey, Peter John
Liberty Orchards Limited

Lewington, John
Brogdale Craft Cider Limited

Lewis, James William
James Lewis Cider Ltd

Lilley, Christopher Stanley Alfred
Lilley's Cider Limited

Lilley, Marc
Lilley's Cider Limited

Lincoln, Darren
Kendal Brewery Ltd

Lindenberg, Frank Karl-Heinz
Bevisol Limited

Lindgren, David Richard
The Cotswold Fruit Co Ltd.

Lipao, Josephine
Manmax Ltd

Longe, Danke
The Core Cider Co Ltd

Longe, Marc Adrian
The Core Cider Co Ltd

Lovering, Anthony James
The Halfpenny Green Cider Co Ltd

Luck, Thomas Adam
Bath Ciders Limited

Lynn, Peter Phillip
Whin Hill Cider Limited

MacDonald, Neil Carlisle
Somerset Cider Solutions Ltd

MacNab, Stuart
Hiram Walker (UK) Limited

MacNeice, Gregory
Mac Ivors Cider Co. Limited

MacRae, Darren
The Southey Brewing Co Ltd

Mahinay, Perla
Incubuzz Ltd

Maltby, Robert Charles
Mr. Whitehead's Cider Co Ltd

Manfre, Jordan
Lost Boys Brewery Ltd

Mann, James
Duckchicken Limited

Marshall, Ian Scott John
Lyne Down Organics Limited

Martin, Stephen William
Duxford Scrumpy Co Ltd

Maslin, James William
Jars Cider Ltd

Maslin, Roy Edward
Jars Cider Ltd

Mason, Adam
The Appletreewick Cider Co Ltd

Mathie, Paul Robert
Hoar Cross Cider Ltd

Mathie, Siobain Tara
Hoar Cross Cider Ltd

May, Louise Anne
Alewife and Brewster Ltd

May, Peter Robert
Alewife and Brewster Ltd

McCall, Jonathan
Ginsecco Ltd

McCarney, Stephen Lawrence
Broughton Ales Limited

McClelland, Jodie
Polaners Ltd

McCoy, Luke Laurence
L. McCoy Drinks Limited

McCrindle, James Alistair
Craft Cider Limited

McCusker, Thomas Michael
Magners GB Limited

McDonald, Simon Francis
Lancashire Cider Limited

McGhee, Mary Rose
Hartpury Heritage Trust

McGowan, David Andrew
Broughton Ales Limited

McGrath, Anthony Gerard
The Kinross Brewery Limited

McKay, Conor
One Swan Ltd

McKeever, Patrick
Long Meadow Cider Ltd

McMackin, James Generald
Alcohol Beverages Co Ltd

Melville, Antony Richard David
Tiddly Pommes Ltd

Meyer, Gregory Alan
The Sussex South Downs Co Ltd

Meyer, Oonagh Jane
The Sussex South Downs Co Ltd

Milton, Christopher
Thatchers Cider Co Ltd

Minchella, Sarah
Sephylia Ltd

Mitchell, Fergus Giles Anthony
The Cotswold Cider Co Ltd

Mitchell, Jason
Ashridge Cider Limited

Mitchell, Rosanna Laura
Sibling Winery Limited

Mitchinson, Christopher Thomas
The Crossroads Brewery Limited

Mittler, Stephen John
Cider Brandy Ltd

Moffat, Thomas Dodds
The Kinross Brewery Limited

Monge, Christen Andrew
Kingscote Winery Ltd

Montgomery, James David Keith
The Kinross Brewery Limited

Morgan, Alun David
Cornwall Cider Co. Limited

Morland, Victoria
Liberty Orchards Limited

Morris, Darren John
Celtic Marches Beverages Ltd
Marches Bottling and Packaging Ltd

Morris, James Neil
Parsonage Farm (Croscombe) Ltd

Morris, Nicola Jane
Parsonage Farm (Croscombe) Ltd

Morrison, Angus Kennedy
AA & D Limited
Caledonia Cider Limited

Morshead, Christopher Hurle
Harnser Enterprises Ltd

Morton, Robert Everett
The Bottle Kicking Cider Co Ltd

Morton, Tracey Joanne
The Bottle Kicking Cider Co Ltd

Mount, Camilla Lucy
H.Mount & Sons Limited

Mount, Mark Donald Crichton
H.Mount & Sons Limited

Mount, Rosemary Helen
H.Mount & Sons Limited

Mount, Sam Alexander
H.Mount & Sons Limited

Munro Ferguson, William Hector Luttrell
Highland Cider Limited

Murray, Alan William, Professor
Malton Cider Ltd

Murray, Andrew
Green and Pleasant London Ltd

Murray, Craig John
Festival Beverage and Property Services

Nagaoka Newton, Natalie
Oast Ventures Limited

Nahajski, Piotr Jan
Hampshire Downs Fine Cider Co Ltd

Nash, Matthew Stuart
Old Tree Brewery Ltd

Nashnush, Tarik Ali
House Brewery Limited

Nathan, Steven Jeffrey
Distell International Holdings Ltd

Nattrass, Mark Stephen, Dr
Tremayne Food and Drink Ltd

Naughton, Sean
SMSNaughton Ltd.

Neal, Frank Richard
Renegade Wines Limited

Needham, Leanda Daphne
Scrumpy Wasp Limited

Needham, Timothy Paul
Bad Apple Cider Limited
Grumpy Wasp Ltd
Scrumpy Wasp Limited

Nelson, Eric Frank
Brewers Folly Brewery Ltd.

Nentwich, Oliver
Duxford Scrumpy Co Ltd

Newall, Christopher James Howard
Bevisol Limited

Newell, Christopher John
Wye Valley Meadery Ltd

Newell, Matthew David
Wye Valley Meadery Ltd

Newing, Kevin John
Kingswood Cider Limited

Newman, Thomas George
Mabinogion Mead Co Ltd

Nicoll, Lynsey Jane
H P Bulmer Limited

Nightingale, Peter Alan
Nightingale Cider Co Ltd

Nightingale, Samuel Patrick
Nightingale Cider Co Ltd

Nolte, Werner
Angola Beverages Holding Co Ltd
Distell International Holdings Ltd

North, Simon Paul
Laughing Ass Brewery Ltd

Norton, Keith Richard
The Dower House Cider Co Ltd.

Noyce, Vincent Robert Amos
The Portsmouth Distillery Co Ltd

O'Connor, Peter George
Vachery Farm Cider Limited

O'Sullivan, Colleen
Duckchicken Limited

Olali, Odi
Crosby Beverages Ltd

Oldroyd, Jamie Simon
Apple Hoarders Limited

Oliver, Thomas Richard
Oliver's Cider and Perry Ltd

Olivier, Charlotte
Napton Cidery Limited

Olivier, Jolyon Charles
Napton Cidery Limited

Olliver, Gray Bensted
Branded Drinks Ltd

Oneill, Christopher John
The Shrewsbury Cider Co Ltd

Orbello, Mary Grace
Ginomine Ltd

Osborne, Nigel Richard
The Long Ashton Cider Co Ltd

Owen, Ralph David James
Ralph's Cider Ltd

Palmer, Anthony John Cleeves
Dorset Orchards Limited

Palmer, Cleeves William Robert
Dorset Orchards Limited

Palmes, Chistopher James
Marches Bottling and Packaging Ltd

Palmes, Christopher James
Celtic Marches Beverages Ltd

Panton, Leon
Levscreps Ltd

Parker, James
Loxley Cider Limited

Parry, James William
The Wessex Wild Plum Co Ltd

Parton, Lynda
Pomona Orchards Ltd

Parton, Richard, Mr
Pomona Orchards Ltd

Paterson, Rebekah Sasha
Ostlers Cider Mill Limited

Pattison, Steven Clark
Tempted Cider Co Ltd

Payne, Kevin
Dudda's Tun Ltd

Payne, Robert John
Dudda's Tun Ltd

Pearson, Michael Justin
Pearsons Ciderworks Ltd

Percival, Adrian Maurice
Jaspels Anglesey Craft Cider Ltd

Percival, Janet Iris
Jaspels Anglesey Craft Cider Ltd

Perry, Andrew
Perry's Cider Limited

Perry, George Henry John
Perry's Cider Limited

Perry, Jonathan Henry
Perry's Cider Limited

Philbin, Michael
Ashover Cider Co Ltd

Phillips, Alistair David
Pips Cider Limited

Phillips, Barry Jon
The Meanwood Brewery Ltd

Phillips, Diane Susan
Pips Cider Limited

Phillips, Graeme
The Meanwood Brewery Ltd

Phillips, Richard Bakewell
Monkey Shed Estate Brewing Co Ltd

Pickering, Harry
Pickers Cider Limited

Picton Tully, Ceri
Bygumpty Limited

Picton, Ann
Bygumpty Limited

Picton, William, Dr
Bygumpty Limited

Pike, Sally Jane
Orchard Origins C.I.C.

Porter, William
Spreyton Press Ltd.

Pozzi, Andrea
Magners GB Limited
The Orchard Pig Ltd

Price, Richard John
H.Weston & Sons Limited

Pring, Nicholas William
Marsh Barton Farm Cyder Ltd

Pritchard, Michael Brian
Cornwall Cider Co. Limited

Pryce, Levi
Levscreps Ltd

Puttock, Phoebe
Samba Cidra Ltd

Rafter, Michelle
Ashover Cider Co Ltd

Ramirez, Rhiena
Adhinton Ltd

Read, Harry George
Sadler-Wilson & Read Ltd

Reed, Simon John Lees
Goodness Sake Limited

Reeve, Jaqueline
Marley and Barley Ltd

Reeve, Stephen Charles
Marley and Barley Ltd
The Peasmarsh Cider Co Ltd

Reid, Carl
Batch Cider Ltd

Reid, Giles Nicholas
South Downs Cider Limited

Reynolds, Richard David Leonard
Barbourne Perry Limited

Reynolds, Suzanne Ginevera
Barbourne Perry Limited

Richmond, Arthur William
Merrydown PLC

Rippon, Matthew Bennett
Creoda's Hill Ltd

Ritsema, Benjamin Lee
Cranes Drink Ltd

Ritsema, Daniel James
Cranes Drink Ltd

Roberts, Garreth Samuel
Ancient Wine and Beverages Ltd.

Roberts, Simon
White Rose Cider Limited

Roberts, Theresa
Gwatkin Cider Co. Limited

Robertson, Ewan James
Gaymer Cider Co Ltd

Robinson, Alan William
H & A Prestige Bottling Ltd
Halewood International Limited

Robinson, Angus Charles
Robinsons Cider Limited

Robinson, Charlotte Louise Clifton
Rock Hill Cider Co Ltd

Robinson, Dickon Hugh Wheelwright
Rock Hill Cider Co Ltd

Robinson, Nicholas Robert John
Robinsons Cider Limited

Robinson, Robert Charles Christian
Robinsons Cider Limited

Robinson, Susan Kinloch
Robinsons Cider Limited

Rogers, Dave
The Garden Cider Co Ltd

Roldan, Emilia
Halorank Ltd

Rolfe, Danielle Marie
Penton Park Brewery Limited

Rolfe, Guy William
Penton Park Brewery Limited

Ross, Helen Elizabeth
Goodness Sake Limited

Roubaud, Marc
Aston Manor Limited

Roy, Alan John
The Kinross Brewery Limited

Rudge, Mark Andrew
Wasted Apple Co Ltd

Rutter, Mark Christian
Ancient Wine and Beverages Ltd.

Ryan, Jonathan Ashley
Pembrokeshire Cider Limited

Ryan, Richard Henderson
Tempted Cider Co Ltd

Sadauskas, Antanas
Neptune SA Ltd

Sadler-Wilson, Finlay
Sadler-Wilson & Read Ltd

Sahota, Davinder Singh
Holler Brewery Limited

Sandall, Robert Charles
Thatchers Cider Co Ltd

Sandbach, David Alastair Douglas
Wimborne Cider Co Ltd

Sanderson, George
Lost Boys Brewery Ltd

Sandrini, James Alexander
Revenant Cider Limited

Sawit, Albert
Covenflare Ltd

Saxby, Amanda Jane
Saxby Farms Limited

Saxby, Philip John
Saxby Farms Limited

Scales, John
The Radnage Cider Co Ltd

Scarcella, Amy Louisa
Lines Brew Co Ltd

Schulz, Timothy
Colourful Outbursts Limited

Scoley, Helen Rose-Marie
Westmoor Botanicals Limited

Scoley, Philip George
Westmoor Botanicals Limited

Scott, Joseph Lewis Bartholemew
Wide Eyes Enterprises Limited

Sealey, Ryan Ray
Caledonian Cider Co Ltd

Sebastian, Sarah Monica
Onefolks Ltd

Selby Bennett, Andrew Charles
Cidre Bouche UK Limited

Sells, Patrick David, Dr
Horse Kick Cider Ltd

Sharman, Mark Richard William
Sharpham Wine Limited

Sharp, Dougal Gunn
AA & D Limited

Sheppy, David James
Sheppy's Cider Limited

Sheppy, Louisa Naomi
Sheppy's Cider Limited

Shipman, Craig John
Toby's Cider Limited

Shipman, Karen Elizabeth
Toby's Cider Limited

Showering, Jonathan
Showerings Cider Mill Ltd
Brothers Drinks Co. Limited

Showering, Matthew Herbert
Brothers Drinks Co. Limited
Showerings Cider Mill Ltd

Sikorsky, Radovan
H P Bulmer Limited

Silcock, David
Highworth Cider and Perry Ltd

Simpson, Beth Nadine
Peak Ciders Limited

Simpson, Neil Allan
Hawkes Cider Limited

Sitwell, William Ronald Sacheverell
3CS Cider Limited

Skinner, Steven John
Cornwall Cider Co. Limited

Skyner, Anna
Eastern Cider House Ltd.

Slater, Daniel Christie
The Kinross Brewery Limited

Sloan, Joseph
Merrydown PLC

Smith, Alan
White Rose Cider Limited

Smith, Antony Paul
House Brewery Limited

Smith, Cameron Robertson
The Husthwaite Orchard Village Ltd

Smith, Cindy
Ross-on-Wye Cider & Perry Co Ltd

Smith, Daniel Keith
Sibling Winery Limited

Smith, Guy Christopher
Somerset Cider Co Ltd

Smith, Jordan
Jordan's Car Review Ltd

Smith, Martin William
Broxbourne Brewery Ltd.

Smith, Patrick James
Sibling Winery Limited

Snowden, David Philip
The Berkshire Cider Co Ltd
Crazy Dave's Cider Ltd

Sobey, Priscilla Jane Hardwicke
Haygrove Evolution Limited

Souter, Rory Julian
Boho Cider Ltd
The Cotswold Cider Co Ltd

Spiers, Ludovic
Aston Manor Limited

Spry, Simon Mark
Spryder Ltd

Stanier, Norman John
Haygrove Evolution Limited

Staughton, Simon James
Bath Ciders Limited

Stead, Dominic
House Brewery Limited

Stephens, Paul Benjamin
Primeflow Limited

Stevens, James Richard
Essex Cider Co Ltd

Stevens, Jonathan David Philip
The Garden Cider Co Ltd

Stevens, Wayne Russell
Loxley Cider Limited

Stewart, Fina
Bridge Farm Cider Limited

Stewart, Nigel Ian
Bridge Farm Cider Limited

Stuart, Peter Neilson
Thistly Cross Cider Co Limited

Studley, Todd Matthew
Secret Orchard Cider Ltd

Sumog Oy, Donna Mae
Evopan Ltd

Swaine, Jonathon David
Cornish Orchards Ltd

Tait, Gavin
The Donhead Apple Co Ltd

Tant, Oliver Reginald
The Copse House Cider Co Ltd
Landshire Cider Ltd

Tatton, Alastair Charles
Umbrella Brewing Limited

Tayburn, Lee Andrew
H & A Prestige Bottling Ltd
Halewood International Limited

Taylor, William
Kentish Maid Ltd

Taylor-Welsh, Kelly
H P Bulmer Limited

Thackray, Christopher James
Craftwater Brewing Co Ltd

Thatcher, Martin
Thatchers Cider Co Ltd

Thomas, Helen Maureen
H.Weston & Sons Limited

Thomas, Richard
Bhat Ltd.

Thomas, Samuel Fraser
Angry Coot Fermentation Co Ltd.

Thompson, Evan Peter
Mount Bank Farm Limited

Thompson, Geoffrey James
The Lambswick Drinks Co Ltd

Thompson, James Digby
The Lambswick Drinks Co Ltd

Thompson, Nathan Edward
The Clandestine Distillery Ltd

Thompson, Rupert Geoffrey Ryland
Thatchers Cider Co Ltd

Thompson, Sarah
The Boutique Cellar Limited

Thompson, Stephen Robert
Umbrella Brewing Limited

Thompstone, Andrew
Thompstone Industries Ltd.

Thomson, Brendan
Renegade Wines Limited

Thorne, Anita
Proasset Limited

Thornton, Fraser John
Distell International Holdings Ltd

Tinston, Liam
Tinston Wines & Ciders Limited

Tizon, Carla
Aohimetron Ltd

Todd, Gary Alexander
Thomas Hardy Burtonwood Ltd

Todd, Iain
The Kingston upon Hull Liqour Co Ltd

Topp, James Herbert
New Forest Cider Limited

Topp, John William Henry
New Forest Cider Limited

Topp, Mary Louise
New Forest Cider Limited

Topp, Sally Anne
New Forest Cider Limited

Topp, Susan Daphne
New Forest Cider Limited

Toseafa, Caroline
Caxdon Premier Limited

Toseafa, Donald
Caxdon Premier Limited

Tranter, Paul Albert
Symons Cyder & Fruit Wine Co Ltd

Treacy, Conal
Scott's Irish Whisky Ltd

Troughton, Helen Elizabeth
Armagh Cider Co Ltd

Troughton, Mark
Armagh Cider Co Ltd

Troughton, Philip Samuel
Armagh Cider Co Ltd

Tully, Steven Richard
Bygumpty Limited

Turpin, Vincent
Hiram Walker (UK) Limited

Uprichard, David James
Tempted Cider Co Ltd

Uprichard, Janet Estelle Barnett
Tempted Cider Co Ltd

Vaughan, Susan Jeanette
Celtic Marches Beverages Ltd
Marches Bottling and Packaging Ltd

Venour, Richard James
Apple Anarchy Limited

Villaroman, Myla
Infirock Ltd

Vizcarra, Kathleen Ann
Drapex Ltd

Volschenk, Leonard Jacobus
Distell International Holdings Ltd

Voss, Neil Mark
Thomas Hardy Burtonwood Ltd
Thomas Hardy Holdings Limited
Thomas Hardy Kendal Limited

Wady, Christopher
Wadys Cider Limited

Wagstaff, Michael David
Chalice Mead Limited

Wale, Lucy Catherine
Tutts Clump Cider Ltd

Wale, Timothy Gilbert
Tutts Clump Cider Ltd

Walgate, Benjamin James
The Peasmarsh Cider Co Ltd

Walker, Philip Lawrence John
The New Union Brewing Co Ltd

Walsh, Martin
Bevisol Limited

Waltham, Elizabeth Eve
Haygrove Evolution Limited

Wang, Bowei
Overtone Brewing Ltd

Ward, Giles Duncan
Tees Cider Ltd

Ward, Jonathan Christopher
Thomas Hardy Burtonwood Ltd
Thomas Hardy Holdings Limited
Thomas Hardy Kendal Limited

Ward, Margaret Rae
Thomas Hardy Burtonwood Ltd
Thomas Hardy Holdings Limited
Thomas Hardy Kendal Limited

Ward, Mark Jonathan
The Regal Rogue Group UK Ltd

Waterton, Corrine Elaine
The Harrogate Cider Co Ltd

Waterton, Paul
The Harrogate Cider Co Ltd

Watkins, Jonathan Steven
Spinney Abbey Ltd

Watson, Russell James
East Norfolk Trading Co Ltd

Watson, Sally
East Norfolk Trading Co Ltd

Watt, James Bruce
Hawkes Cider Limited

Watts, Philippa Jo
Kingswood Cider Limited

Webber, David Paul
Bullington End Cider Limited

Weeks, Joseph Paul
Moss Cider Limited

Weston, Henry Norman
H.Weston & Sons Limited

Weston, Timothy John Hubert
H.Weston & Sons Limited

Whewell, James Robert
Little Teapot Ltd

White, David
Himachal Ltd

Whitehead, Alexander
Mr. Whitehead's Cider Co Ltd
Mr. Whitehead's Drinks Co Ltd.

Whittock, Craig Aaron
The Viking Winery Ltd

Wickens, Gary Christopher
W & W Drinks Ltd

Wilce, Brian Maurice
The Ledbury Cider and Juice Co. Ltd

Wilce, Peter Robert
The Ledbury Cider and Juice Co. Ltd

Wilcox, Abigayle
Wibblers Brewery (Farms) Ltd

Wilcox, Adrian
Orchard Origins C.I.C.

Wilcox, Jeremy John
Wibblers Brewery (Farms) Ltd

Wilcox, Philip John
Wibblers Brewery (Farms) Ltd

Willett, Alisdair James
Apple Hoarders Limited

Williams, Brett John
Twin Barrel Brewery Limited

Williams, James Scott
The Lovely Cider Co Ltd

Williams, Richard
Revenant Cider Limited

Wilson, Robert
Bio Slim Health & Energy Drinks Ltd
Lamson Wine Co Ltd

Wise, Paula
Wise Owl Cider Ltd

Wise, Richard John
Wise Owl Cider Ltd

Woodcock, Margaret
Black Dog Meadery Ltd

Woolley, Deb
Harleston Cider Co Ltd

Woolley, Deborah Vine
Hiken Limited

Woolley, Ken
Harleston Cider Co Ltd

Woolley, Kenneth John
Hiken Limited

Woolley, Tim
East Coast Cider Co Ltd
Harleston Cider Co Ltd
Heaton Cider Co Ltd

Worledge, Christopher
Ham Hill Cider Limited

Worledge, Simon
Ham Hill Cider Limited

Worley, Neil John
Worleys Cider Limited

Worsey, Simon
Darley Abbey Cider Co Ltd

Wright, Simon Joseph
Hawkes Cider Limited

Wright, Stephen Charles Richard
Old Chads Orchard Ltd

Wyatt, Richard Anthony
W & W Drinks Ltd

Yntema, Yde Bouke
Analytical-Solutions UK Ltd

This page is intentionally left blank

Standard Industrial Classification

excluding

Manufacture of cider and other fruit wines

01210 Growing of grapes
H.Mount & Sons Limited

01230 Growing of citrus fruits
Crai Cider Co Ltd

01240 Growing of pome fruits and stone fruits
Analytical-Solutions UK Ltd
Cooks Cider Ltd
Damsons in Distress Limited
Frampton Farm Limited
Hoar Cross Cider Ltd
Liberty Orchards Limited
H.Mount & Sons Limited
Old Chads Orchard Ltd
H.Weston & Sons Limited

01270 Growing of beverage crops
Crai Cider Co Ltd
Sibling Winery Limited
Spryder Ltd

01300 Plant propagation
Lyne Down Organics Limited

01420 Raising of other cattle and buffaloes
James Lewis Cider Ltd

01450 Raising of sheep and goats
Frampton Farm Limited
Lyne Down Organics Limited
Parsonage Farm (Croscombe) Ltd

01470 Raising of poultry
Parsonage Farm (Croscombe) Ltd

01500 Mixed farming
Medlar Management Limited
Mount Bank Farm Limited
H.Weston & Sons Limited
Wibblers Brewery (Farms) Ltd

01630 Post-harvest crop activities
Appledunc Limited
Damsons in Distress Limited

10320 Manufacture of fruit and vegetable juice [14]
Analytical-Solutions UK Ltd
Bensons Fruit Juice Limited
Cotswold Fruit Co Ltd.
Crosby Beverages Ltd
Dean Press Cider Ltd.
Handmade Cider Co Ltd
Hidden Orchard Ltd
Liberty Orchards Limited
Little Teapot Ltd
Neptune SA Ltd
Orchard Origins C.I.C.
Tiddly Pommes Ltd
W & W Drinks Ltd
Wasted Apple Co Ltd

10390 Other processing and preserving of fruit and vegetables
A Little Luxury Distillery Ltd
Tiddly Pommes Ltd

10710 Manufacture of bread; manufacture of fresh pastry goods and cakes
SMSNaughton Ltd.

10840 Manufacture of condiments and seasonings
Handmade Cider Co Ltd
Harleston Cider Co Ltd
Tremayne Food and Drink Ltd

11010 Distilling, rectifying and blending of spirits [30]
A Little Luxury Distillery Ltd
Angola Beverages Holding Co Ltd
Boutique Cellar Limited
Brothers Drinks Co. Limited
Broughton Ales Limited
Clandestine Distillery Limited
Cool Brew Dept Ltd
Damsons in Distress Limited
Distell International Holdings Ltd
Ginsecco Ltd
Holler Brewery Limited
Kendal Brewery Ltd
Kingston upon Hull Liqour Co Ltd
Lamson Wine Co Ltd
Liberty Orchards Limited
Ludlow Vineyard Limited
Marron (Lincoln) Ltd
Neptune SA Ltd
New Union Brewing Co Ltd
One Swan Ltd
Penton Park Brewery Limited
Portsmouth Distillery Co Ltd
Rock Hill Cider Co Ltd
Saint Patricks Ltd
Salcombe Cider Co Ltd
Sky Pirate Ltd
Solway Spirits Ltd
Southey Brewing Co Ltd
Still Wild Limited
Zymurgorium Ltd

11020 Manufacture of wine from grape [23]
AB Vaults Group Limited
Alcohol Beverages Co Ltd
BF Wines UK Ltd
Boutique Cellar Limited
Broadland Wineries Limited
Caxdon Premier Limited
Clandestine Distillery Limited
Cool Brew Dept Ltd
Creoda's Hill Ltd
Embev Ltd
Flower Miners Limited
Kingscote Winery Ltd
Lines Brew Co Ltd
Ludlow Vineyard Limited
Luminati Wine Limited
Medland Manor Vineyard Ltd.
Noahs Estate Ltd
Polgoon Vineyard Ltd
Sharpham Wine Limited
Sibling Winery Limited
Tinston Wines & Ciders Limited
Tremayne Food and Drink Ltd
Wild Life Botanicals Ltd

11040 Manufacture of other non-distilled fermented beverages [25]
Angola Beverages Holding Co Ltd
Bitter & Sweet UK Ltd
Cool Brew Dept Ltd
Crossroads Brewery Limited
Dampney's Remarkable Drinks Ltd.
Distell International Holdings Ltd
Fruito Soft Drinks Limited
Ginsecco Ltd
H & A Prestige Bottling Ltd
Halewood International Limited
Thomas Hardy Burtonwood Ltd
Thomas Hardy Holdings Limited
Thomas Hardy Kendal Limited
Hawkins Drinks Limited
Kingston upon Hull Liqour Co Ltd
Last Sign Brewing Co Ltd
Little Wolf Brewing Limited
Old Tree Brewery Ltd
One Swan Ltd
Saint Patricks Ltd
Sky Pirate Ltd
Tremayne Food and Drink Ltd
Wasted Opportunity Limited
Westmoor Botanicals Limited
Zymurgorium Ltd

11050 Manufacture of beer [51]
Alcohol Beverages Co Ltd
Angry Coot Fermentation Co Ltd.
Aston Manor Limited
Boutique Cellar Limited
Branded Drinks Ltd
Brewers Folly Brewery Ltd.
Broughton Ales Limited
Broxbourne Brewery Ltd.
Brute Brewing Co Ltd
Clandestine Distillery Limited
Craftwater Brewing Co Ltd
Crai Cider Co Ltd
Crosby Beverages Ltd
Crossroads Brewery Limited
Thomas Hardy Burtonwood Ltd
Thomas Hardy Holdings Limited
Thomas Hardy Kendal Limited
Hawkins Drinks Limited
Holler Brewery Limited
Jordan's Car Review Ltd
Kendal Brewery Ltd
Kinross Brewery Limited
Last Sign Brewing Co Ltd
Laughing Ass Brewery Ltd
Little Teapot Ltd
Little Wolf Brewing Limited
London Beer Co Ltd
Long Ashton Cider Co Ltd
Lost Boys Brewery Ltd
Mad Yank Brewery Ltd
Marourde Limited
Meanwood Brewery Ltd
Missing Link Brewing Ltd
Monkey Shed Estate Brewing Co Ltd
New Union Brewing Co Ltd
Old Town Brewery Ltd.
Old Tree Brewery Ltd
One Swan Ltd
Overtone Brewing Ltd
Thomas Paine Brewery Limited
Penton Park Brewery Limited
Sky Pirate Ltd

The UK Cider Industry

Solway Spirits Ltd
Southey Brewing Co Ltd
Ten Tors Brewery Ltd
Twin Barrel Brewery Limited
Umbrella Brewing Limited
W & W Drinks Ltd
Westmoor Botanicals Limited
Wibblers Brewery (Farms) Ltd
Zymurgorium Ltd

11060 Manufacture of malt
AB Vaults Group Limited
Brewers Folly Brewery Ltd.
Fruito Soft Drinks Limited

11070 Manufacture of soft drinks; production of mineral waters and other bottled waters [25]
AB Vaults Group Limited
Ashridge Cider Limited
Crosby Beverages Ltd
Fruito Soft Drinks Limited
Ginsecco Ltd
Handmade Cider Co Ltd
Thomas Hardy Burtonwood Ltd
Thomas Hardy Holdings Limited
Thomas Hardy Kendal Limited
Hartpury Heritage Trust
Hawkins Drinks Limited
Hidden Orchard Ltd
Kendal Brewery Ltd
Kingston upon Hull Liqour Co Ltd
Marley and Barley Ltd
Merrydown PLC
Moss Cider Limited
Mr. Whitehead's Drinks Co Ltd.
Neptune SA Ltd
Pembrokeshire Cider Limited
Saint Patricks Ltd
Salcombe Cider Co Ltd
Showerings Cider Mill Ltd
Westmoor Botanicals Limited
Wild Life Botanicals Ltd

14190 Manufacture of other wearing apparel and accessories n.e.c.
Conte International Limited

26400 Manufacture of consumer electronics
SMSNaughton Ltd.

30300 Manufacture of air and spacecraft and related machinery
Harnser Enterprises Ltd

31090 Manufacture of other furniture
SMSNaughton Ltd.

33160 Repair and maintenance of aircraft and spacecraft
Harnser Enterprises Ltd

41100 Development of building projects
Cornish Mead Co.Limited

43999 Other specialised construction activities n.e.c.
Scrumpy Wasp Limited

45111 Sale of new cars and light motor vehicles
Levscreps Ltd

45200 Maintenance and repair of motor vehicles
Medlar Management Limited

46170 Agents involved in the sale of food, beverages and tobacco
Branded Drinks Ltd

46341 Wholesale of fruit and vegetable juices, mineral water and soft drinks
Woodstar Limited

46342 Wholesale of wine, beer, spirits and other alcoholic beverages [22]
A Little Luxury Distillery Ltd
Angola Beverages Holding Co Ltd
BF Wines UK Ltd
Batch Cider Ltd
Branded Drinks Ltd
Broadoak Cider Co Ltd
Broughton Ales Limited
Bumble Mead Ltd
Craftwater Brewing Co Ltd
Distell International Holdings Ltd
Flower Miners Limited
L'Atypique Ltd
Lamson Wine Co Ltd
Laughing Ass Brewery Ltd
Lilley's Cider Limited
Monkey Shed Estate Brewing Co Ltd
Noahs Estate Ltd
Organic Country Drinks Ltd
Scrumpy Wasp Limited
Sharpham Wine Limited
Solway Spirits Ltd
Wild Life Botanicals Ltd

47110 Retail sale in non-specialised stores with food, beverages or tobacco predominating
Broadlands Cider Farm Limited
Harleston Cider Co Ltd

47250 Retail sale of beverages in specialised stores
Bio Slim Health & Energy Drinks Ltd
Brogdale Craft Cider Limited
Lamson Wine Co Ltd
Organic Country Drinks Ltd
Sharpham Wine Limited

47410 Retail sale of computers, peripheral units and software in specialised stores
Levscreps Ltd

47710 Retail sale of clothing in specialised stores
Oast Ventures Limited

47810 Retail sale via stalls and markets of food, beverages and tobacco products
Bio Slim Health & Energy Drinks Ltd
Noddy's Cider Ltd

47910 Retail sale via mail order houses or via Internet
Levscreps Ltd

47990 Other retail sale not in stores, stalls or markets
Woodstar Limited

51102 Non-scheduled passenger air transport
Harnser Enterprises Ltd

52103 Operation of warehousing and storage facilities for land transport activities
Festival Beverage and Property Services

55209 Other holiday and other collective accommodation
H.Mount & Sons Limited
Mount Bank Farm Limited

56102 Unlicenced restaurants and cafes
Cairn O'Mohr Ltd.

56103 Take-away food shops and mobile food stands
Conte International Limited

56210 Event catering activities
Marley and Barley Ltd
Meanwood Brewery Ltd
Missing Link Brewing Ltd
Moss Cider Limited

56302 Public houses and bars
Festival Beverage and Property Services
Last Sign Brewing Co Ltd
Meanwood Brewery Ltd
Missing Link Brewing Ltd

59111 Motion picture production activities
Thompstone Industries Ltd.

62090 Other information technology service activities
Old Chads Orchard Ltd

68100 Buying and selling of own real estate
Conte International Limited

68209 Other letting and operating of own or leased real estate
Festival Beverage and Property Services

70229 Management consultancy activities other than financial management
Analytical-Solutions UK Ltd
Broadoak Cider Co Ltd
Donhead Apple Co Ltd
Legiste Limited

71122 Engineering related scientific and technical consulting activities
East Coast Cider Co Ltd
Hiken Limited

74902 Quantity surveying activities
Mount Bank Farm Limited

82920 Packaging activities
Somerset Cider Solutions Ltd

85590 Other education n.e.c.
Lyne Down Organics Limited

86220 Specialists medical practice activities
Medlar Management Limited

94990 Activities of other membership organisations n.e.c.
Hartpury Heritage Trust

96090 Other service activities n.e.c.
Orchard Origins C.I.C.

Printed in 8pt Nimbus Sans L

Designed by URW++ Design and Development GmbH

Dellam Publishing Limited

2 Heath Drive, Sutton, Surrey, SM2 5RP

Fax: 020 8770 7478   email: enquiries@dellam.com

SAN: 0177881   EAN/GLN: 5030670177882